Family Tradition Witchcraft

Kit McGoey

GREEN MAGIC

Green Magic
5 Stathe Cottages
Stathe
Somerset
TA7 0JL
England

www.greenmagicpublishing.com
info@greenmagicpublishing.com

Typeset by Green Man Books, Dorchester
www.greenmanbooks.co.uk

ISBN 978-0-9561886-5-6

GREEN MAGIC

Dedication:

This book is for my wonderful mother, without whom none of this would have been possible (literally!).

Kit McGoey

IV

CONTENTS

Acknowledgements

So many people helped this book come into being. The whole thing has been like a dream come true for me and I am still pinching myself. I'd like to thank Pete Gotto very much, for his encouragement, kind words, and mostly for saying "yes" to publishing this book. I'd like to thank the editor and Jerry the typesetter.

I'd like to thank Jim Pye for many interesting and thought provoking discussions on witchcraft, magick, and the nature of the universe. Rob Johnston, the first male witch outside my family that I ever met (wherever you are these days Rob, your Circle on the lawn at Killie will never be forgotten). Ted Dickson for helping me figure out the blasted computer. I want to thank Chris Cusack for driving me around, listening to my rants, for many favours and for being a great friend. I must thank Melissa, Rob, Jay, Kelly, Ken, Dave, Donato, Casey, Little Danny, Baby, Ric, Emma, and everyone at the Original Motorcycle Cafe for being such a fabulous cheering section. I have to thank Danny and Rachael for solid advice and lots of good times. I want to thank Harry Doupe for his encouragement and for making me laugh so hard beer shot out of my nose.

I want to thank those who have gone before, all of those who were burned or strangled for no good damn reason, and those who were brave enough to keep the secret, keep the flame burning for those of us that came later. I need to thank all the tremendously wonderful contemporary writers who make the subject accessible. I certainly want to thank those in my family who went before me and showed me a way of living that makes perfect sense, Phemie, W.I., Etta, Kitty, Nan, Lottie, and especially Andy. Be you in Summerland or in your next incarnations I hope I have made you proud and said it the way you would have wanted it said.

I'd like to thank my friend Tyler, who although he believes differently always encouraged me and gave me the benefit of his rapier mind.

I need to thank my dearest friend Olivia Whitton and her lovely, warm, smart, generous and beautiful family for their endless patience when I monopolize their wife/mother/daughter for her fabulous mind and great advice.

I want to thank my nephew William and niece Sydney for providing the smiles when they were in short supply and my brother in law Paul for his tolerance in matters that he considers "weird." I have to thank my amazing, wonderful, brilliant sister Alex, for giving me the necessary computer software, for listening to me rant and ramble and worry, for always being there and knowing exactly what I mean. I'd like to thank my Dad, Tom, for being completely supportive of me in everything I've ever tried to do, knowing the logical, reasonable, clever and grown up answer to all my questions, and laughing in the right places. My Mum, the incomparable Nancy, who has taught me basically everything I know. She provides the inspiration, the creativity, the knowhow and barrels of love.

I hope I haven't forgotten anyone. Most of all I'd like to thank my partner in life, in crime, in love, in everything; Bill Dickson. Baby, you're my world, and without you I don't know where I'd be, but I'm certain I wouldn't have the confidence in myself and joy to even attempt to write a book. Thank you for putting up with temper tantrums, a messy house and a noticeable reduction in hot meals while I worked on this book. You're the smartest, sweetest and best man in the world, and I am the luckiest woman.

Introduction

In the middle of the nineteenth century two sisters take ship from Scotland alone. They are only teenagers and they are leaving behind everything they have ever known to start a life free of fear in a new world.....

One of the sisters was my great great great grandmother, Phemie. She arrived in Ontario, Canada at the tender age of sixteen. Although she came from a well-off family her parents could not protect her anymore from rumours and the lunacy that accompanied witchcraft persecutions in the 1800's. She had always been "strange" or "fey", given to visions and sneaking out past the servants to be in the woods alone at night. Those servants were whispering and word reached her parents that finally it was going beyond talk. That something was going to be done about their daughter, the witch. So with heavy hearts they prepared their daughters to leave them. Phemie travelled with her sister, a servant couple, and a not insignificant amount of money to begin another life in safety.

Once in Ontario Phemie met a man she fancied named W.I. Although he was already married, they had a friendly relationship. He was a respected Scottish engineer, new himself to Canada.

Etta:

Born in 1863 great great Grandmother Etta lived to be nearly 94 years old. Her nickname among the extended family was "Gypsy." At the age of sixteen she lost the lower part of her leg when she slipped under a train in icy conditions while returning home from a party. Self conscious about her walking she was allowed to elope, and many stone paths were built around Killiecrankie for her convenience. Her spare wooden leg remained in Killiecrankie's attic until the end, providing a thrill for children. The loss of her leg may have lent to her incredible creativity in outlets of painting, knitting, wood carving and furniture design. She is remembered as discussing current affairs, people, religion and politics with a broadmindedness and tolerance uncommon to the times well into her 90's. The day before her death, Christmas Day 1956 she stayed up late playing Scottish Ballads on the piano, and the next morning with an example of the Sight called for her daughter to come over and be with her, holding her hand as she passed.

When, sadly, his wife perished in childbirth along with the child, he and Phemie married and named their first daughter Margaret as a memorial to his first wife. It was an exciting time for the couple. They were well-to-do and W.I. had a good career. He worked on the Thames embankment, among other projects, so they lived in London for a time and they travelled to other places for leisure, owning two houses in Tallahassee, Florida and a house in Toronto, Ontario. They would have seven children in all, including my great great grandmother Etta, and "Aunt Kitty," a known wise woman.

The family referred to themselves as theosophists, a religious form of mysticism which was all the rage at the time, the objects of which include investigating the unexplained in Nature and the powers latent in humankind. Theosophists had a very progressive attitude toward woman, as well as another fine objective, which was to form a Universal Brotherhood among all people regardless of creed, colour, race or sex. Some people consider the modern day New Age movement to be based on Theosophical teachings. Even in the new world one couldn't openly declare oneself a witch. Although they faced economic depressions and several times came close to losing their fortune through no fault of their own, Phemie is repeatedly credited with somehow (magickally?) gathering together resources and seeing them through until they made their fortune again. They were always seekers, exploring, pushing the boundaries of what was acceptable and searching for knowledge, even making a family journey to Japan only a few decades after it was open to westerners in search of new forms of magick and occult learnings. They returned with silks, slippers, curios and purloined Japanese Iris bulbs, which at the time were not available to the public and which grew in the garden of their summer home for over one hundred years afterward.

Around this time, early in the 1880's, Phemie became friends with Dr. Emily Stowe, one of Canada's first female doctors. They were suffragettes together in Toronto where Emily had finally been granted a license to practice medicine from the Ontario College of Physicians and Surgeons in 1880. Before this, Emily had to go to New York in the 1860's to learn medicine and be granted special permission in 1870 to attend the Toronto School of Medicine. When she first applied to the University of Toronto the President of the University is said to have stated "The doors of the University of Toronto are not open to women, and I trust they never will be." She is said to have replied, "Then I will make the business of my life to see that the doors of the University will be opened and that women may have the same opportunities as men." She had a special interest in herbal and homeopathic remedies prompted by the need to treat her husband who contracted tuberculosis in 1863. Dr. Stowe's group of forward-thinking women was originally called 'the Women's Literary Club,' so that they could meet to discuss tactics without stirring up public outcry. The group was instrumental in getting such privileges for women as separate public bathrooms and stools for women clerks to sit on. Later, the group changed its name to the 'Women's Suffrage Association,' and campaigned for women to have the vote, as well as influencing the University of Toronto to finally open to women during the 1886-87 year. Emily's daughter Augusta went on to become the first female physician licensed in Canada, and in marrying another doctor became half of the first married couple of doctors in the country. Throughout this time Phemie and Emily were close, and Emily was the attending physician at almost all family births. Emily's values and views were similar to my own family's, particularly regarding the equality of women. It was Emily who told Phemie about the magick of Muskoka, Ontario.

In Muskoka there is special lake, now called Lake Joseph. Long treasured by First Nations peoples for its healing properties, there are tales of Native Medicine People bringing their sick and injured by travois or other means to be bathed in its rejuvenating waters. By the 1880's Muskoka was beginning to be developed as a resort area. People were discovering the rocky soil was useless for farming but that their health was better when they escaped the humid, dirty city of Toronto during the hot summers. Phemie, her sister, W.I., and their children visited "Stowe Island" for several weeks in the summer of 1885 and bought a large plot of land directly across the lake the following summer. It had been farmed and the family hurried to re-forest it. By the time I grew up the land was filled with birch, beech, maple, oak, elm, basswood, cedar, pine, spruce, and one rare black walnut tree. The original piece of land was about 18 acres and purchased for around $1600. Over the years the property would be sub-divided into at least eight lots where additional cottages were built for all the children and their families. In my day we had a whole shoreline of relatives in both directions and the family was often referred to as "the colony," or "the clan." Phemie and W.I. brought eight carpenters over from Scotland to build their octagonal summer home. These men built the kitchen wing, a separate structure, first and lived in it while working on the main section. Built before electricity with all hand tools, it was somewhat of a marvel on the lake, constructed in sections and then raised at once, appearing suddenly one day where there had been nothing the day before. All the hardware was iron, known for its protective qualities, and some of the flawed, original window panes were still there in the 1990's. The first known octagonal structure was an ancient Temple in Greece that housed the Oracle at Delphi. Phemie and W.I. chose an octagonal structure as it was fashionable at the time, received more natural light, was cooler in the summer, and because it was as close to a circle as was possible for them to build. Their home would be a magick circle where their four daughters held séances and explored the occult. It was called Killiecrankie.

It was three stories high, originally white with red trim, brown for a time and then white with black roofs in my day. People said it looked like a wedding cake. A deep wrap-around veranda provided the choice of sun or shade the whole day through and the distinctive pattern that all the railings had is a useful design for the border of written spells. The boys lived in the attic; the help in a snug room behind the kitchen, the separate building that helped keep the main house cool. Off the dining room there was a long closet with a false back and secret room for hiding in case the burning times ever returned. The living room walls held family pictures and artwork, a stag's head that was very old, and magick swords that were used often in circle casting. On top of the attic roof was a flagpole that often flew a special enchanted Killiecrankie flag and the "Widow's Walk," from which you could see nearly the length of the lake. It was surrounded by gardens and forests teeming with wildlife.

My great great Aunt Kitty, who inherited Killiecrankie from her parents Phemie and W.I., was "single by choice," as she put it. She spent her springs, summers and autumns at Killiecrankie, tending the huge perennial garden, "doing charms" for a niece's baby or a nephew's new job, playing the piano, and spending time with her relatives, especially her sisters, including my great great grandmother Etta, a wood carver who created beautiful carvings, some of which remain in family homes and on public display. Aunt Kitty was in tune with the natural world and observed the seasons with private rituals, deciding only toward the end of her long life to share some of her knowledge with a select few. She was by all accounts a stern and somewhat forbidding woman, but also very fair-minded and large-hearted. Dinner was served at a table on the veranda, rain or shine, with fine china. She often served guests a (somewhat unpleasant) drink of blackcurrant preserve and hot water which she swore was beneficial to health. Boys from up and down the shoreline were charged with bringing water by bucket up the long hill from the lake to water her garden. At an advanced age in a nursing home she confounded all the staff by asking repeatedly for her "horn," which was finally discovered to mean a nightly tipple. She eventually chose a grand nephew who had shown her the most

The four sisters left to right: Peggy, Lottie, Etta, and Kitty.

respect for her way of life and beloved home to inherit her house
and private beliefs. She gave Killiecrankie to my grandfather for
one dollar and "love and affection" and bestowed much secret
knowledge upon him after observing his abilities to control the
weather, make the gardens flourish and know what people were
thinking and feeling. His own mother, my great grandmother,
had married a bank president and hid her knowledge and magick
talents to blend into "society" better. Her magick was regarded
more as "parlour tricks" to amuse party guests.

Great great grandmother Etta and Aunt Kitty passed on in

the early 1950's, but my mother remembers them from when she was a small girl, mostly by virtue of their great presence and the huge respect they garnered from her father and all the family. Aunt Kitty returned to Killiecrankie for a few summers after giving it to my grandfather but she was saddened by the modern conveniences he installed, such as plumbing, and died not long after. My mother learned much herbal and weather lore and "family secrets" at the knees of her great aunts and more still from her father, one of the family's only male witches to date. Mostly the family had baptized the children as Anglican for proprieties' sake and kept much of the secret knowledge from any outsiders, who could mean anyone outside the core group, and indeed from the men. We have definitely always been a matriarchy.

My mother is an extraordinary woman with a great deal of power. As teenagers all my friends sought her out for advice and if they wanted a boy to notice them it was always "Please do a spell for me, Mum!" (They all called her "Mum" too) I have learned so much, and continue to learn from her. She is naturally closed-mouthed on the subject of witchcraft, perhaps from growing up in a time when it was still seriously frowned upon, and also perhaps because she believes one should learn as much as they can for themselves. But she taught me love magick, garden spells, how to call up a storm and much more. We continue to study and practice the Craft together. My father, while not magickal, has always been open minded and supportive. I have been, and am, very lucky.

Growing up I spent all my summers at Killiecrankie. We had huge parties every Litha, inviting everyone on the lake. I was told at a very young age to remember to tell everyone that it was a "solstice party" and nothing more. The Japanese Iris' planted by my great great great grandmother still bloomed every spring and it was known if you wanted to strengthen your marriage you could dig up a bulb, dry it, grind it and add it to your charm. Fiddleheads collected in the early spring were lucky and made a delicious meal steamed with a little butter. Rare types of hummingbirds visited the feeder at the kitchen window every summer. Flowers and herbs for love, luck, prosperity, protection, and spirituality grew in different garden patches all over the property. If it was still and hot my grandfather could be prevailed upon to "whistle up a wind" although mostly he would tell you to go for a swim in the lake first. Conversely, if the weather turned nasty it was known that you would be safe in the house as it was "a circle" and boats caught out in bad storms landed frequently at our dock to take shelter. Smokey, milky, and crystal quartz stones could be found along the shore simply by picking up a handful of pebbles and were known to be "naturally clean" and in no need of cleansing before use. At Lammas (or the "August long weekend") and Mabon ("Our Thanksgiving") we had bonfires, great roasts, vegetables, herbs and loaves of bread and gave our thanks for nature's bounty. If you were feeling poorly you knew to add a handful of mint from the kitchen garden to your tea. The good weather returned when "Sister South Wind" began to blow in the city and Beltane was the time to open the Killiecrankie for the season with feasting and celebrating around the maypole (which masqueraded as a bird house holder when not in use), on the back lawn. If a strong east wind started to blow however, we would pack up and head for the city just like Phemie in the 1800's.

Our journey back to Toronto took about 2 hours by car, whereas it was a day trip by train and steamship before the highway from the city was built in the 20's and the road to our door went in the 1950's. This ease of access may have been what stole the magick from Muskoka. Nowadays cottages are crammed in cheek by jowl, the lake is full of speedboats and jet skis, the frogs have all but disappeared. In my mother's day there were crayfish, beaver and salamanders, by my day it was rare to see a turtle. The first time I saw a black squirrel in the nearest town, early that last summer, I knew the end of an era was at

Killiecrankie Circa 1952

hand. The squirrels in Muskoka had always been red or grey before. Cottages on Lake Joe routinely sell for over two million dollars. Muskoka is the "in" place for Toronto's well-to-do and Killiecrankie is gone. On July 9th, 1999 an electrical fire sparked in the old wood and burned the attic and part of the second floor. Maybe our protective spells had worn thin, or maybe we took for granted that all the descendants, "the clan," would fight for Killiecrankie, but we went to court alone. My mother and sister and I didn't seek out the trendy who's-who group, and didn't belong to the country club set. We kept to ourselves and perhaps the extended family thought we didn't want their help. To the uninitiated perhaps we seemed strange. I vividly recall one incident of a cousin calling the police and telling them we were running a bawdy house after observing some friends and I casting a circle on the lawn as teenagers. A greedy relative who had turned her back on magick and witch craft and wanted a "normal life" had control of Killiecrankie through a Power of Attorney and a sick grandmother. After the fire, despite articles in the local paper, despite the Historical Society's pleading, despite the fact that there was enough insurance money to more than cover the repair, we lost. The land was sold and the magick home of seven generations demolished.

For a time after that I turned my back on magick and witchcraft. It was as though a beloved relative had been killed. The sadness was almost unbearable. Killiecrankie was forever, a "family trust," a constant in all our lives for 113 years. It wasn't so long before that we had had the huge 100 year reunion when relatives came from everywhere and celebrated together. Over 200 hundred family members and 50 friends came that day in 1986. I can remember my grandfather's intense joy at being the "laird," wearing a kilt, having a haggis piped in. Gazing at the group photo of that reunion as a young girl I can recall touching my finger to the faces of those who "knew the secret," a small inner group. Plans for the 125th anniversary were already being discussed. As I write this in 2011 I realize that reunion would have been this summer. There are still some "clan," members along the shoreline in both directions from where Killiecrankie once stood, but we do not hear from them often. I am only glad my grandfather did not live to see the betrayal of this relative, and those who did not fight to save the "family trust," or it surely would have killed him.

But after a few years, as the sting began to lessen, I felt magick calling to me. It is in my blood, surely. Maybe it is in my very DNA after all those generations of witches. They fought hard against the laws that kept women down and against the rules of a society that did not accept their right to practice their beliefs openly. They kept it alive even when they had to flee their homeland, even when they were afraid of being ostracized or even burned. So I began to realize I owed them something and that I couldn't ignore what they had done. That now, in this enlightened age when witches can have their own magazines, their own section in the bookstore, their own websites, can go on TV and talk freely about the Goddess and the Sabbats and the old ways that I should share what I know. So here is my Grimoire. I have faithfully tried to reproduce all I have been taught and all I have observed. I hope you will enjoy it. I have learned something as I began to practice again and as I write: Witchcraft comes from within. It doesn't depend on any special location or fancy trapping. No matter what happens it is there inside you, and even if the past is shattered it is always there to sustain you. Blessed Be!

1: A WITCH'S WORLD

What is a witch? The dictionary gives a few different definitions which include "an ugly or mean old woman, a hag," or a "female sorcerer or magician," or "a being, (usually female) presumed to have special powers from the devil." Hmm. Not very appealing, or very accurate! The origin of the word witchcraft is Middle English, dating from before 900 AD and may have come from "wicce craft," the original definition of which is said to be "The Craft of the Wise," a term still used today. Even among witches, Wiccans, and neo-pagans there are different answers. Some use the definition that a witch is someone able to attract and control unseen forces. Others suggest that if you have always been attracted to animals, rain storms, night time and nature you could be a witch. Wiccans follow a more formal belief system that always includes the worship of the Goddess and God. Some continue to identify with the Christian (or other) religion and practise witchcraft or spells and charms "on the side." In my family we were all baptized as Anglican but some of us had a special inclination toward something more, something different.

Among those that had this inclination an even smaller subset are (or were) seekers who pursued it and adopted another religion: witchcraft. Even in my own family group the definition of "witch" can be hard to nail down. Witchcraft could be defined as a religion that is nature based, like paganism, but with the addition of spell casting, Goddess and God worshiping, Sabbat observing, charm making, circle casting, and may often include some degrees of herbalism, gemology, crafting, healing, divination and other disciplines. But there is more to it than simply that. A witch is someone in tune with the seasons and cycles, with those around her or him, with nature, animals, and the weather. A witch is, as I said a seeker, someone who searches the past and the future, someone who is deeply responsible and works at constant self-improvement.

I have heard it spoken and read it more times than I can remember in countless variations that there is more witchcraft in a spider web, in a thunderstorm, in quiet places, in dew on leaves, in a cat's purr or dog's play or a loved one's arms, than any book or any degree. Yet I still want to put what I can in this book in the hope that it inspires even one person to take it further or helps someone learn some things they didn't know. Witchcraft may be difficult to define even for those who practise it but it is a very definite feeling, a way of living and looking at life, and once you are involved in it you will certainly feel it and know it. You may, in time, come up with your own description of the religion or belief system that is exactly right for you.

Who are witches? Today there are witches and Wiccans (more on that later) in all walks of life all over the world. Studies have suggested that forms of neo-paganism including Wicca are among the fastest growing religions as people become disenchanted with patriarchy and search for something with more personal meaning. In almost every language there is a word that translates to "witch," be it the Italian Strega, the Russian Koldoonia, the Spanish Bruja, the Greek Magissa, the Latin Saga, the Cambodian Mi Thmop, or the Icelandic Vitka. Not all of these words have very nice meanings, although for the most part people today, especially in the Western world are more open minded and accepting of different beliefs. Of course, it was not always so. Even the most casual lay person is aware of the witchcraft persecutions, the Burning Times, or the Salem Witch Trials.

Once upon a time, before the rise of the "big three" patriarchal religions (Christianity, Judaism, and Islam) nearly everyone was pagan. The word comes from the Latin 'paganus,' meaning 'rustic,' or 'country-dweller.' Today neo-pagan is a blanket term that covers many belief systems including Wicca, shamanism, Native American belief systems, and other nature-based religions. Before the patriarchy became so prevalent, paganism was simply what everyone practised. They had the same Goddesses and Gods and fire festivals to celebrate the seasons in the country and the cities. In the country the people worshipped under the sky and needed no priest or temple to talk with their deities. Among the pagans in Europe at least (and probably everywhere) there was a smaller group of 'wise women or men,' or 'cunning women or men,' who would have had specialized knowledge, including herbal wisdom useful for healing and the ability to cast spells or make charms. They would perhaps have done divination and communicated with ancestors and spirits, and known about stones, the stars, and the seasons. We will call them witches for clarities sake. They are often likened to the clergy as against the general population of parishioners. They would have been respected for their abilities and learning, and sought out for help in times of need.

Things began to change at some point, although it is hard to put an exact date on it. There is some evidence that contributors to the Old Testament were, in 550 BC, the first to suggest the stoning of witches. The Old Testament features such passages as Exodus 22:18 "Thou shalt not suffer a witch to live," and Leviticus 20:27 which basically states that a man or woman with a familiar spirit or who is a wizard shall be stoned. That was only the beginning.

A persecution followed; a scourge that lasted many centuries and is not completely over today. Constantine I was the first Roman Emperor to convert to Christianity, and issued the Edict of Milan in AD 313 which was designed to restore and keep order and stop fighting among traditional pagans and new Christians. The Edict stated that all people should be free to practise faiths of their choosing including Christians. All well and good, if only things could have stayed so tolerant and accepting! In 420 AD Augustine suggested that witchcraft was impossible and the pagan people were in error in their belief in any power that did not come from God. Paganism and Christianity did continue to co-exist for some centuries, but Christian missionaries were very zealous. In order to make conversion more palatable many pagan festivals were incorporated into Christian practise. For instance Yule, December 21rst, the shortest day of the year when we promise ourselves that light will return became the birth date of Christ, a fine time for revels in the bleak winter (Many theologians and historians suggest that the Jesus' actual birthday was sometime in March). Ostara, the Spring Equinox turned from the rebirth of the Sun (or the God) into the rebirth of the Son with Easter.

However, it seems that the Church of Rome was not satisfied with the conversion rates they were getting. At some point they decided that all competitors or even anyone who chose to believe something different must be totally stamped out. We have the Crusades, so blood soaked they are hard to contemplate, the persecution of the Cathars (who were suggested to be devil-worshippers in 1208 AD, perhaps where the idea that devil worship was an effective slander came from) the eradication of the Knights Templar, and the witchcraft oppression (it is fair to say that Jesus himself who advocated love and peace might have been horrified by the bastardization of his message). Pope Gregory IX established the famed and bloody Inquisition to deal with non-Christian activity in the early 1230's AD (although he personally did not advocate torture). In AD 1273 Thomas Aquinas, a Dominican monk, put forth the idea that demons "reap the sperm of men and spread it among women," starting the idea that demons were real and had the desire to corrupt humankind, as well as starting up ideas of unusual and sinister sex practises among certain factions of the population. In 1450 many captured Cathars admitted to the use of witchcraft under torture and the Church began to define the so called "evil" practises they wanted to subvert.

In 1484 Pope Innocent the VIII announced that satanists in Germany were having meetings with the devil and causing crops to fail. After Heinrich Kramer, a Dominican Inquisitor asked for the authority to persecute witches Pope Innocent VIII issued a Papal Bull (Summis Desiderantes Affectibus) that organized and regularized the oppression. Kramer and Jacob Sprenger wrote and published the "Malleus Maleficarum," (Maleficarum is a Latin word meaning 'wrong doing,' or 'mischief,' and generally referring to malevolent magic) 'The Hammer of Witches,' or 'The Witches Hammer.' This terrifying document refuted prior claims that witchcraft didn't exist, explained that most witches were women who got up to dreadful things and was used to educate magistrates and other authorities on methods of pursuit and conviction of witches. Among other outrageous ideas the Maleficarum suggests that female witches collect and keep twenty to thirty male members in a birds nest in a tree and infers that orgies and pacts with the devil are common (does this sound a bit like some men were feeling emasculated by powerful women and those men wanted to take that power away from women?) At this time there was a prevailing feeling that some people (witches) possessed special knowledge and power and this was no longer considered beneficial. These abilities were now believed to come from the devil and therefore be heretical and go against the rule that there should be no power but from the one true God. The Church now stated that Christians had an obligation

17

to pursue and destroy witches. The Maleficarum is an interesting read and definitely worth a look; it would almost be humorous if one could forget the bloodshed it led to. Reprinted copies are available today over the Internet.

From the year 1480 to the year 1750 it is estimated that between 40 000 and 100 000 men, women, and children were executed for witchcraft in Europe. About seventy to eighty percent of them were female. That was certainly one way to virtually eliminate powerful women, the Goddess, and people making magic and having control of their fates outside of the Church and its teachings. Not to mention all the valuable land, personal possessions and money that became property of the Church when its owners were executed. Women in these times in Europe were mostly considered the property of their husbands or fathers and had very few rights whereas once they had been venerated (have a look at images of Palaeolithic stone carvings of the ripe female form, the Goddess of fertility from which all life springs). The year 1515 saw some 500 witches burned at the stake in Geneva Switzerland. One thousand were executed in Como Italy in 1524. In 1591 King James of Scotland authorised the use of torture on suspected witches and it was widespread in other nations. An accused man from the Court of Charles IX of France in 1571 announced that he had some 100 000 fellow witches in his country which fuelled massive hunts and executions there. Although torture was not allowed in England to extract confessions Matthew Hopkins, an extremely feared witch judge travelled the country between 1645 and 1647 teaching sleep deprivation and other techniques, such as "dunking," or "ducking," where the accused were immersed in bodies of water. If they sank (and died) they were pronounced innocent, but if they floated they were killed, the rationale (if you can call it that) being that they had rejected their baptism so the water was rejecting them. Many who were tried and convicted probably considered themselves Christian, whether they practised some herbology or spells or made some charms or not. A person might be convicted on the basis of having a 'witches mark,' such as a third nipple or mole, and might be accused simply for having a pet cat. The death of animals, the failure of crops and any kind of sickness often began a mad frenzy of witch hunting.

In 1682 the last witch, Temperance Lloyd was executed with two other women in England, and in Scotland Janet Horne was the last witch executed in 1727. By this time many prominent figures were criticizing the executions and the methods used to obtain convictions. In 1735 a final Witchcraft Act in Great Britain led to prosecutions for fraud rather than supernatural powers and was often levied against Roma (gypsies) and fortune tellers. The attitude that witchcraft did not exist was back. The final witchcraft laws in Great Britain were repealed in 1951. In the new world about 150 people were accused in the Massachusetts colony and about 40 were executed. The New England witch hunt lasted from 1648 to 1663, while the Salem witch trials were later, taking place in 1692 and 1693 in several villages around the colony. One man refused to plead either way and was crushed under heavy stones to attempt to force him to do so.

We are very lucky to live in more enlightened times, although witch hunts still continue in some form in places such as Papua New Guinea and Cameroon. We now have a freedom people have not had for a millennium. Today there are occasional stories of a witch not getting a job because of his or her religion and the like, but for the most part we are free now to practise as we please. Most people I have encountered are merely curious on the subject, but many modern day witches choose to remain "in the broom closet." Certainly I am the first in the family to speak about our "secret" publicly. We have always been reserved about speaking of it, even to one another and many of our rituals contain little or no vocalizing, just thoughts and visualization. How much did the men in my family before my generation know? I suspect they knew quite a bit. It's hard to conceal a balefire on the lawn at midnight! As to whether sleeping draughts were ever used I cannot say but I think not. More likely they kept a "need to know" attitude. We have long been a matriarchy, yet life was good for the men. W.I. always had enough money from his wife even when business ventures went south, and he had beautiful children and a lovely life. His attitude, and that of the following generations was no doubt something like, "Why rock the boat?"

So what is witchcraft like today? We understand that in the past a witch may have been a village herbalist, a wise one called on to remedy a fever or interpret a dream, but how does that apply in a modern world? Of course witchcraft has evolved over the centuries, and much ancient sacred knowledge was forever lost. We walk a line of resurrecting what we can from the past and creating a modern tradition that makes sense in this day in age. As in the past we have problems that we want to take steps to remedy and a desire to understand our place in the world. Today there are many branches of witchcraft. They all fall under the inclusive term of neo or contemporary pagan. Pagans generally practise nature-based religions and believe in a life force present in all natural things, called 'Animism.' To understand the difference between witches and pagans the example is often used that while all Baptists are Christian, not all Christians are Baptist. The same is true for witches and pagans: All witches are pagans, but not all pagans are witches. Witches use magick and cast spells. Among witches there are different groups too. Right now there is the large (and ever growing) religion of Wicca, whose followers are called Wiccans.

Modern Wicca is generally attributed mostly to Gerald Gardener and his followers and compatriots, one of whom was Aleister Crowley. Doreen Valiente, a member of his group, wrote the famous Charge of the Goddess that many work with today. There are many other notable branches of Wicca such as Alexandrian. Modern Wicca has its roots in the twentieth century and is more and more popular every day. There are countless good resources available to educate oneself on Wicca. Wiccans worship a Goddess and God, often in archetype form (see *A Witch's Goddess and God*) and celebrate eight Sabbats a year. Some people consider the words 'witch' and 'Wiccan,' to be interchangeable and suggest that Wiccans have simply rejected a term with negative connotations. There are many that do not agree with this. Although Wicca is a beautiful religion and it always wonderful to see the Old Ways come back to the light in whatever form, there are variances between my family's form of witchcraft (and other traditional practitioner's witchcraft) and Wicca. Many practitioners of Wicca have strived very hard to cast their religion in a benevolent light, and some folks think it a bit watered down. Modern books on Wicca rarely mention the Great Rite for example (see *A Witch's Sex Magick*) or they sometimes suggest that spell work is mostly a form of prayer, which is quite different from my family's beliefs.

Wiccan adherents follow the Wiccan Rede: "Eight little words a witch's rede fulfil: an' it harm none do what thou will". (there are several similar forms). This is a great rule to follow, but growing up we did not have it. It has not been proven to pre date the 1940's, although "Do what thou Will shall be the whole of the Law," and its response "Love is the Law, Love under Will," appears in a work of Crowley's from 1904. It is interesting to note that while the Rede is treated as law among adherents the word "rede" means "counsel" or "advice," rather than any absolute. 'Do what thou will' does not mean do whatever strikes your fancy, it means do what your will dictates. Finding your will, your true own self and wisdom is an integral part of the path.

If the Rede is the ethical consideration for Wiccans, what kind of ethics do other witches follow? Does being a witch mean you can curse whoever you want to obtain whatever you desire? Hardly! We were raised with a variation of the Golden Rule: 'Do onto others as you would have them do onto you'. While this is similar to a Biblical passage it is interesting to note that the

Golden Rule and its companion the Silver Rule (the negative, such as `Don`t do to others what you would not like done to you') exist in different forms throughout recorded history. Ancient Egypt, dating from the Late Period (664-323 BC) had "That which you hate to be done to you, do not do to another", and Ancient Greece had "Do not to your neighbour what you would take ill from him."

Ethics in witchcraft (and Wicca) are deep and many layered. Students of Wicca are encouraged to meditate on the Rede and explore its deeper meanings and all its ramifications, such as 'harm none' including oneself. Many branches of witchcraft subscribe to a belief in Karma; the eastern philosophy which holds that for every event that occurs another event will follow that is based upon the first. That next event will be unpleasant or pleasant based on the first event. Karma also holds that nothing happens to a person that she or he does not deserve (this is a very general summation of a very interesting philosophy that certainly bears further study by those interested). Other witches believe in the three-fold law, that whatever energy you send out into the universe, the universe (or the deities) will return to you times three. Therefore if you spend a lot of time cursing people and wishing them ill it will return to you in unpleasant (and unforeseen) ways. You will be much happier and more fulfilled if you spend your energy on positive work. Wiccans tend to focus only on the positive aspect of magick, and this may well be for you. Others believe that a witch who can't curse can't cure. Wiccans often speak of "white magick," whereas many witches state that there is no white or black magick, only shades of gray. The nature of the intention is known only in the heart of the witch that is certain. In my family tradition the emphasis is on you as the witch to be responsible for your every action and to consider all the implications of your activities. Would you be okay with this is if someone did it to you or for you? If so, then it is almost always all right.

Responsibility is another edict that is very important to all witches, be they Wiccan or not. Witchcraft teaches us that we must take complete responsibility for ourselves. We never rely on "cop outs" such as "the devil made me do it." There is no devil and we alone control our behaviour. We do not look to others to excuse ourselves for anything we have done. No matter what type of childhood you've had, or adversary you have faced, you must seek to rise above it. We look after ourselves, and conduct ourselves with honour. We believe in the interconnectedness of all things and that we are a part of nature, not separate from it. We like to observe nature, it gives power. It's good to be quiet and think, and spend some time alone. It's important to realize the vastness of the universe yet know you have a place in it, and endeavour to learn what that place is. Be true to yourself always. Another thing that characterizes witches is a desire to take an active role in life rather than letting it wash over you. If you don't like your situation or how things are going you can take steps to change it through the aid of spells and magick. Witches are not passive. If something is wrong we take steps to fix it with whatever means are at our disposal, and magick is one of our tools.

Most witches believe in re-incarnation, that our souls are on a learning journey that may last many lifetimes. Many believe that souls rest for a time between lives in a place often called 'Summerland,' and that this resting time may last for long periods, even centuries. In our tradition we believe that we choose what family we are born into, we decide before birth where to go so that we may re-incarnate with the same souls including lovers. We believe that our choice is also based on a desire to learn the most that we can in each incarnation and mature as souls. Many witches feel that karma can carry over from past incarnations and it is best to try not to leave things unfinished in this life.

Today as in times of old there are two types of witch or Wiccan, solitary or coven member. This is a deeply personal choice. Covens nearly always work on initiation principles with a degree

23

system, usually three degrees lasting a year and a day each, but it varies. Working in a group can be vastly rewarding and powerful, plus you can learn a great deal in a coven setting, being taught by like minded people with a lot of experience. Initiations into traditional covens have great merit and power. The very repetitive nature of the spoken phrases has power and the charged belief surrounding them gives them strength. Remember though that no one can ever tell that you are not a witch because you do not have a degree to hang on the wall or you haven't gone through "the" initiation. You know inside yourself what you are. If you are interested in joining a coven most large Western cities have them and many rural areas too. The Internet is a good place to start both to locate a coven in your area and to decide which one might be best for you as they vary greatly; some are longer established and some are more formal etc.

Solitary practice is by no means lesser. In my family we were less formal. I was considered a witch after several years of study and practice but there was no formal ceremony of my initiation. I am what I was born to be, and my teachers, namely my mother, grandfather, and some of the "young aunts," had a hands-off approach. There is a lot of really great material for self study out there today and a lot of junk too. You may have to wade through some junk to find things that are meaningful to you and give you a greater understanding and a feeling of connection. It can be lonely practicing alone or with one or two others but there is power in it too. In the quiet of night with just you and the moon you can hear your own inner voice better and you can release any self-consciousness and simply be yourself, which is often the first step on the path. Witchcraft is a path as much as a religion, one we walk all our lives without reaching the end. A witch is always learning, and even a third degree initiate has not "arrived" at any final destination. There is always room for more growth.

Is what we practice today the same as what our pre-Christian ancestors practiced? Naturally witchcraft has evolved over the centuries and adapted. There were those that attempted to preserve the Old Ways, keeping it hidden, keeping the secret. Very little would have been written down as these writings would have been a death sentence during the Burning Times and few rural cunning women (or men) would have possessed paper and ink anyhow. What we were before Christian times most likely had different wording and even slightly different tools. I am truthfully not sure when my family tradition began. Who taught Phemie what she knew? Perhaps her mother, perhaps someone else in Scotland brought her in to the Old Ways. Certainly she learned much more throughout her life, as we all try to do. Would I like to believe that what I practise comes down in a pure, undiluted, and unbroken line from pre-Christian times? Of course! More likely though, a great deal of what I have been taught comes from the occult revival of the nineteenth century. Sometimes things change spontaneously as well, and that can be a great thing. There is great power in a verse that has been repeated dozens or hundreds of times with the same intent, and great power in the base sympathetic magick and charm making the village wise woman would have practiced, so anything truly old is wonderful to use when we can find it. In the twenty-first century we are resurrecting something, adapting something, remembering something. There is power in the new, power in belief, and power within each of us as well. Most of us believe the essence of witchcraft, the heart of it is unchanged since time immemorial.

That essence is what we are all seeking all the time in witchcraft, the magick in waves on a beach, in a crackling fire, in the wind in the trees, in the cycles, in ourselves. Now we are really free to be ourselves and cast off patriarchy completely. There is no longer any need to be one thing to the priest and another in the field. It really is *magickal* when you slip beneath the surface and begin to realise the power that lies there. When you step onto the path and your journey begins you will be (or perhaps have been,) amazed. This book, like any other on the subject is a primer. It is a guide to help you align your mind in such a way to open it for the experience of witchcraft, a Mystery which has to be felt and lived. If this Mystery is for you, I invite you to step onto the path and walk it (or continue walking it), for it is a fulfilling and wonderful journey. Witchcraft gives you the power to really change your reality, and change your life for the better.

2: A WITCH'S GODDESS AND GOD

Deity concepts are probably as old or almost as old as humanity itself. It has been suggested that humans are the only species aware of their own limited life spans, and as such have always tried to make sense of the universe and what our purpose might be. Primitive religions sprang up when we were still only hunter-gatherers and evolved alongside our societies. It can be argued however, that deity concepts are still primitive. Among our tradition there are those that wonder if we can ever come close, at least at this stage in our evolution, to understanding the cosmos and who or what created them and us. Were we created at all? Do we have a purpose? How can we ever know for sure? The answer to that of course is that we cannot. Perhaps someday science and technology will come closer to explaining more of the Great Mysteries of this universe but for now we cannot be one hundred percent sure. That is where faith comes in.

More blood has been shed over faith and religion than over any other conflict. Different Gods seem to get people fired up like nothing else. Religious wars continue, even today, in a supposedly civilized world. There was a time though when many cultures across continents seemed to agree on something: The Goddess. Neolithic stone carvings are the basis for much of our supposition about ancient European religion; many detailed statues of ripe female figures have been uncovered by archaeologists. But beyond that we can see a trend among many peoples: Greek, Roman, Celtic, Aztec, Assyrian, Phoenician, Egyptian, Slavic, Huron, many African peoples, Chinese, Japanese, Iroquois, Norse, Hebrew, Inuit, Sumerian, Indian and many others have worshipped Goddesses. This makes sense when we consider the history of humanity, how as we transitioned from hunter-gather societies to agricultural ones the Goddess became an even more important part of daily life. She was most likely appealed to for help, and blessings for fertility of crops and animals, as well as intercessions with life's hardships. She was probably a nurturing and loving divinity for the most part, although she would have a dark side too from which come storms and other natural upheavals.

This is another subject on which we can never be positive. Some cultures have preserved their Goddesses but many have not. The histories, especially of prehistoric Europe are simply too fractured, and those who came after too determined to obliterate all traces of the Mother Goddess. It seems the rise in patriarchal religions and their inherent desires to cultivate, subdue, and subvert both the land and anyone who stood in the way of their domination wiped out the Goddess and her followers fairly thoroughly, or so they thought. For centuries Mary was so dear to people that in 431 AD at the Council of Ephesus she was officially named the Mother of God and people were allowed to worship her, although not as a deity. However, Mary is so beloved by so many, it begs the question is there a real need in people to have a female deity in their lives? I believe so. Lately we are seeing a resurgence of Goddess worship and the feminine divine and this is wonderful on so many levels. But there are those that are so involved with the Goddess, the power of women, and unshackling themselves from millennia of oppression by patriarchy that they want no part of the God or the male aspect.

There are several forms of deity worship; Polytheism, the belief in many Gods (and Goddesses), Pantheists, who believe that God and the universe are the same thing, Panentheists, who believe that God contains the universe but is not the universe (a view held by many Theosophists, as well as some Neo-Pagans, Hindus, and Kabbalah followers), and Monotheists, who believe there is only one God. In some cases Monotheists believe that many different religions are worshipping the same God only under different names, which is a very interesting thought, and similar in form to what some Wiccans believe; that all Goddesses (and Gods) are one. However Monotheism has led, at different times throughout history to a belief that a certain group are "chosen people," or posses an "absolute truth," which can, of course, lead to conflict.

Neopagans, Wiccans, and witches for the most part believe in a dialestic or dualistic form of deity, namely a male and female aspect, a Goddess and God. In my family tradition this is partially a result of a desire to personify different energies present in the universe. There are opposite polarities present all over the place, night and day, light and dark, new moon and full moon, high tide and low tide, birth and death, male and female. In our minds it only makes sense that there would be two governing forms of energy of opposite natures, comparable to male and female. Maybe we do not even understand the first thing about deities or creators but there will always be a hankering to make them relatable, accessible, and familiar. You might ask ten different witches about their ideas of the Goddess or God and get ten different answers. She might be a beautiful, rounded woman at the height of pregnancy holding a sword, an ancient woman with a long silver braid and a knowing smile, a bare breasted huntress accompanied by wolves. He might be a man whose face is made of leaves who appears in the forest, a gnarled grandfather who would place his hand on your head in times of trouble, a young boy with shining eyes and a sweet smile. None of these is incorrect in any way. The Goddess and God may appear differently to each person, according to their pre-conceived notions, or if they have been lucky enough to know them more intimately through visions, dreams or meditations. It helps to be able to picture them in your mind when you are trying to communicate with them. There are many images on the Internet and in books if your imagination needs a boost. To me the Goddess or Mother Nature is a ripe full-bodied woman (why would a Goddess ever starve herself when there is so much to be tasted and enjoyed?), who usually wears a serene smile unless roused by an injustice, and the God or the Green Man is virile looking, wild and strong, but with a wise, kind face. You may have totally different ideas on the matter of course, and these ideas may change as you become more familiar with your deities or at different stages throughout your life.

Many Wiccans and witches consider their Goddess and God to be archetypes. An archetype can be loosely defined as an original or prototype on which all things that follow are based on, or a quintessence, i.e. the archetypal bachelor. Carl Jung further elaborated on the concept of archetypes, explaining that an archetype can be considered to be a pattern of thought or an image that is present in all individual psyches. Commonly reoccurring archetypes include the Hero, the Trickster, the Mentor, and the Wise Old Woman or Man. The concept of our deities as archetypes is an interesting one and allows modern day Wiccans to include the old Goddesses and Gods under one umbrella, believing them all to be forms of one, or actually two great deities.

On the other hand, some peoples such as Celts would be taken aback by this notion. To many people the Gods and Goddesses have defined individual personalities, whole pantheons worth.

Different members of these pantheons govern different things, such as marriage, childbirth, the hunt, war, the harvest and so on. Some covens and solitary Wiccans and witches today are extremely devoted to their chosen or inherited pantheons, such as those of Scottish and Irish descent and the Celtic Gods and Goddesses. Others adopt a pantheon that feels right or resonates with them, such as Egyptian, Greek or Roman.

My own family tradition falls somewhere in between. Growing up I knew about Mother Nature and the Jack O' the Green, as well as the Lord and Lady, the Lady of the Night and her Consort, Mother Earth and the Green Man or Pan. But there were also times when Aphrodite was appealed to for help in love matters or Isis for her special power in boosting a spell. Brid (always pronounced 'Breed') was also a constant presence in our lives, appealed to when we were sick or things were going wrong about the house. Even today no one agrees, or perhaps it is more accurate to say in my family no one knows for certain whether there is one true God and Goddess or a whole group of them. It could be said that while we believe in only one Goddess and God when we appeal to their different names we are appealing to certain aspects of their nature.

Like so much in witchcraft it comes again to personal preference and what feels the best to you, what feels right. If you are going to work within a coven or established group they will most likely have a pantheon that they use, or they may stick with Lord and Lady. For the sake of focus it is important to be consistent within group workings, even if you chose a different form of worship when you are alone. If you are a solitary you will have a completely free rein in your choice. Consider your heritage as a place to start. Many cultures have traditional Gods and Goddesses, such as the Welsh and Irish Morrigan, Kuan Yin of China, Asase Yaa of western Africa, Parvati of India, Diana of Rome, Athene of Greece, Pele of Hawaii, Ataentsic of the Iroquois and Huron peoples, or the Slavic Baba Yaga to name just a very few traditional Goddesses. Among Wiccans and witches the Greek, Roman, Celtic and Egyptian pantheons are especially popular and there is a lot of information available on them, but with research you should be able to find out about many others as well. It is important to study up on your chosen deities and understand them before you appeal to them or call them to your Circle. Some supreme beings have dark sides and you must always be aware and careful of what or whom you summon or invoke.

You may wish to keep it simply to Lord and Lady, Lady and Consort or Goddess and God. This is perfectly all right, many witches and Wiccans do. Sometimes it easiest to see and relate to them as just two beings, one Goddess and one God, who encompass and govern all. As I have said whatever works for you. That is one of the most beautiful parts of witchcraft as a religion, the ability to make choices and decisions based on your own feelings and what makes sense to you or what is comfortable to you. If you choose to simply worship the Goddess and God you will still want to conceptualize what they look like to you and what their natures are. Typically the Goddess governs women, children, most domestic animals and plants, the home, marriage, childbirth, pregnancy and fertility, the moon, water, rain, the night, the stars, love, Earth, friendship, health, and some aspects of prosperity and sex. The God on the other hand is often in charge of most wild animals and places, the harvest, especially of grain crops, the sun, the day, fire, air, many incenses and candles, athames, wands, war, certain plants and trees, some aspects of prosperity, love, sex and health, fathers, men, toil and labour, and hunting. This is the breakdown of their specialities used by my family but you may find many variations. There are likely no right or wrong choices for each as they are ideal partners and work together in almost everything.

Almost all witches, Wiccans, and Neo-Pagans hold that the Goddess has three aspects and is a Triple Goddess. These stages are called Maiden, Mother and Crone and are symbolized by

Triskele symbols and the colours white, red and black. The Goddess is all three at the same time, as is every woman. The triple aspect of a deity apparently makes sense to many people as Christians adopted it in their Father, Son, and Holy Ghost. In some pantheons the Goddess has a different name for each aspect. The Maiden is generally considered to be independent, wild, seeking, exploring, pure but with a sexual nature, playful, fresh, and sometimes introspective or even self-centred. She is associated with spring, birth, first menses, beauty, innocence and young love or "crushes." The Mother is nurturing, compassionate, fierce when trifled with, ripe, clever, intuitive, creative, lusty and loving. She is associated with summer, bounty, sex, pregnancy, giving birth, marriage and maturity. The Crone is wise or even wisdom personified, knowledge, and power. She is remote and can be hard to get to know, but it is certainly worth it. She is associated with autumn, menopause, the afterlife and reincarnation, and the Mysteries and Higher Learning. All three are associated with learning about oneself and the world. Our tradition holds that the God has triple aspects as well, in Son, Squire and Sage. In some traditions the Squire aspect is known as the Father, and in others the God is not a triple being. The Son is a counterpart to the Maiden and so on. The Son is associated with the colour green, youth and impetuousness, young love and adventure. The Squire with the colour blue, maturity, marriage, sex, fatherhood and work. The Sage is associated with the colour purple and the end of the season or life. He is like the Crone, wise and obscure, but the possessor of unique knowledge and understanding. Braids made of silk or other natural cloth of the three colours of the Goddess and God are sometimes placed on the altar or are present at Circles and Sabbats.

The witches' Goddess and God have a unique relationship in that she gives him birth and later as he matures he becomes her lover and consort. This is the symbolism for the Wheel of the Year. The God (in our tradition) is born at Ostara, the spring equinox, and is in his Son aspect. At Litha, or the Summer Solstice, he is mature, the Squire, and they join. He impregnates her with the new spring, himself. At Lammas he becomes the Sage and at Samhain he falls with the last of the harvest. Other traditions have slight variations, sometimes the God is born at Yule, sometimes Imbolc. Sometimes he dies at Mabon or Lammas and these variances are likely to do with different climates. In the southern hemisphere they may be completely reversed, but the principle remains the same. The God is akin to the sun, he comes to us fully for only part of the year. When he is at his height he is mature and a consort for the Goddess, who is eternal. When he dies, he is not gone because he remains within her, and we know he, as the sun, will return. The God is also eternal, and that is where the Oak and Holly Kings come into play. At Yule the Oak King throws down the Holly King, and this is enacted, if possible, at the Sabbat celebration. The reverse happens with the Holly King throwing down the Oak King at Litha. This helps us to remember that The God, embodied by the sun, is never really gone. Some may find the notion of the Goddess giving birth to, and then having a sexual relationship, with the God unpalatable, but it helps to remember that this is a more a symbolic tale to help keep us in tune with the seasons. Some traditions believe that the Goddess originally created the God as a companion and lover. Some say they came into being at the same time. In our tradition neither is more important than the other, but as most of us are women the Goddess sometimes gets more attention, and the God is sometimes relegated to the role of 'Consort'. Yet all of us know both sides, like the concept of yin and yang, are equally important and neither can exist without the other. Some believe that the Goddess also created herself out of chaos or that she simply was. Some of us feel that the deities and indeed, our own planet are a way for the universe to learn about and understand itself.

Evolution is another subject that can cause much controversy.

Religion and science have been butting heads on this one for awhile, neither side willing to give ground. The subject has led to many conversations in my family over the years, the kinds that go late into the night and include a lot of laughs and drink. What we have basically concluded is that the two are not mutually exclusive. It is entirely possible that the Goddess and God placed all the components for life here on Earth and then watched us develop. That being all seeing they knew what would happen, that humans would evolve eventually. Another thing that causes much debate in religion is free will. It is our belief that the Goddess and God give us free will and allow us to make our own choices so that we, and by extension, they themselves will learn. Some enjoy the notion that they point us in certain directions or cause situations to occur that will get us to predestined places. That way we can believe we are fated to, for example, be with a specific person, as the Goddess and God have set it up for us to be together, yet we always have a choice in the matter. Family myth holds that while the deities are considered "all-seeing," they may not see all the possible outcomes of our choices. When we make choices we learn about ourselves and thus they learn about themselves and the universe learns about itself. Possibly, that is the purpose of deities, humanity, and our world: to learn, and raise each other up through sharing knowledge and truths. That and love, of course. Love is perhaps the most important force in our universe. Again, there will be many variations on these ideas, and I can only speak for myself and the witches in my family.

Many people like to have representations of the deities on their altars or at their workings. Sometimes a white candle is used to represent the Goddess and a black one the God, or sometimes they are reversed. There are lots of lovely statues available these days on the Internet or at New Age shops. Representations of The Green Man, the traditional forest God can be found at many garden centres, usually as a wall hanging that depicts a man's face made entirely of leaves, and this is how he appears in many of our visions of him. The God can be shown very basically as an upward facing triangle, the Goddess as a downward facing one. Others consider the elemental representations to suffice for the Goddess and God; she is embodied in the chalice or cauldron and bowl of salt, he in the candle flame and incense smoke or the athame. Traditional symbolic representations of the Goddess in my family include cauldrons, caves, moons, stars, owls, cats, circles, water, spirals, alligators, spiders, bears, butterflies, seashells, earth or salt, clear and milky quartz, lapis lazuli, sapphires, white and blue stones, willows, and many types of flowers, such as roses, hyacinths, and lilies. Symbols of the God include leaves, many types of trees such as pine and oak, pinecones, acorns, the sun, fire, forests, stags, frogs, cardinals, cactus, daffodils, wheat, corn, holly, flint, obsidian, rubies, topaz, knives, swords, antlers, and lightening. Symbols of their duality include wolves, dogs, foxes, hummingbirds, hawks, turtles, bees, suns and moons together, lunar eclipses, thunderstorms, diamonds, emeralds, rose quartz, amethysts, and athames being dunked into chalices or swords into cauldrons. The traditional symbol for the triple Goddess depicts a waxing crescent moon, full moon (circle) and waning crescent moon in a row, touching. Any of these symbols could be present on the altar or at the Circle or Sabbat in actuality or in the form of pictures, drawings or the like. You may, of course, wish to create your own deity symbolism.

Some witches like to develop a truly personal relationship with either the Goddess or God, or ideally both. They pray to them regularly, or do meditations that attempt to commune with them. They do dream magick in the hopes of receiving their guidance, seek their blessings for all their workings and may even have a specialized grace they say at the table to thank them for meals and dedicate them in their honour. A lot of witches like to leave offerings outside in wild places for the deities. This practise varies from leaving apples cut crosswise at Samhain to something placed out after every spell, to weekly offerings fit for royalty. Aside from tailoring these gifts to what you can reasonably afford there is no right or wrong amount to leave out. Some folk leave bowls of milk for the fairies too. In all likelihood animals get most of these offerings, but this serves the Goddess and God as well. If, like me, you currently reside in a city placing offerings out can be tricky. I use a lake I am lucky enough to be close to, but parks are another option, as are food banks, which I believe would be pleasing to the Lord and Lady. The choice is yours. One really nice thing about witches' deities is that there isn't anyone between you and them. You communicate directly with them, without the intercession of any priest, rabbi or the like. They are accessible to you and you can worship them wherever and whenever you like. In a coven the High Priestess and Priest are there, and may possibly help you interpret what the deities are trying to tell you, but this is not a must. I have found worshipping them in nature to be especially rewarding, but no matter where you are you can reach them and they you.

Although by no means a deity I think "the devil," deserves a mention, if only to state that witches do not believe in him, nor do they worship him. Pan, one of the witches traditional Gods bears an uncanny resemblance to him in that Pan is often depicted horned and has goat-like feet. This comes from Christian priests and missionaries attempting to discredit our deities and make them seem evil. The devil is a patriarchal concept and is no more than a "cop-out." "The devil made me do it, I was possessed, a demon swayed my mind," and so forth are not acceptable to witches. Being a witch means being responsible for yourself and your actions. Furthermore, to give evil a name and so much credence is to feed it and give it power. Evil is created by people. While there may very rarely be restless and mischievous earth bound dead there are no such things as demons. Talk of them and "the devil" is akin to stories told to frighten children into behaving and should be given no more credit.

Other witches remain agnostic or even atheist. These people

may have problems becoming Wiccan, as the Goddess and God are central to Wiccan beliefs, but being doubtful about the divine does not automatically exclude you from practising witchcraft. You can still cast spells, be in tune with nature and the seasons, use correspondences, use magick, and even celebrate the Sabbats without any Lord and Lady present. Some people have been so traumatized or disillusioned by organized religions they want no part of any deity. In my family we judge no one and do not presume to preach or ever seek to convert. People must find their own way and do whatever feels comfortable for them.

3: A WITCH'S TOOLS

A Witch uses nature, magick, the elements, the moon, and many correspondences to cast his or her spells and observe the seasons. Much of the Power at a witch's disposal lies in the realm of spirit and can't be seen or touched. However, a witch also uses Ritual Tools to help call, focus, and send magickal energies. In this enlightened age there are countless websites and mail order companies devoted to nothing but a witch's tool kit and there is nothing wrong with making use of these services, as long as you cleanse and purify all your tools before use. I personally find it is better to try and make your own tools as much as possible, or to find them on your own by searching stores, flea markets, garage sales, the woods and even your own attic or basement, but either method of tool collection is perfectly fine. Nor do you need to have each and every tool listed before you can create magick. It may take years to build your set, and this too is perfectly fine. Witches are, of course, very versatile. That being said ritual tools are just that: excellent tools to aid your magickal workings.

Athame

A ritual or magickal knife. Usually black handled, with a double edged blade, but a single edged blade is fine as well. It need not be very sharp. An athame is used for raising energy, for cutting a door in the Circle, sometimes for casting the Circle itself. The athame should not be more than 13 inches in total length, although a Scottish dirk can be used. Some people use a sword instead of an athame, or in addition to one. This is certainly impressive, especially in Circle casting, but not always practical! In many modern day traditions the athame may not be used to cut anything in the physical world and some folk are very strict about this. In my family tradition it is acceptable to use the athame for herb gathering, wand cutting or peeling, and inscribing candles. In days of old it seems unlikely that many witches would have been able to afford a special knife that could not be used for anything in the material world. So I have been taught that as long as the purpose is related to magick the athame may be used, and this does not sully the blade.

The athame can be placed over a photograph during a banishing to "cut" the relationship or tie. Some folk place the athame under a bed during childbirth or healing to "cut" the pain (obviously this is done at home and never in a hospital!). Used to banish negativity. Represents masculine energy and linked with the God, as well as Fire by some. Used to draw magickal symbols in the air or in the earth or salt during spell work. Waved in a clockwise (deosil) circle over a cauldron, charm, talisman, pouch, etc. to raise energy (anti-clockwise or widdershins to decrease or banish). Used to send magick and Power on its way at the commencement of a spell or ritual. Hold the athame in your Power hand (the hand your write with) and point it toward your magickal intention, picturing the Power flowing down your arm, through the knife and shooting from the tip and on its way.

An athame, like most tools, absorbs energy from use. Handle

it often and bathe it in the light of the Full or waxing moon. You can even engrave, or have someone engrave, personal and magickal symbols on the blade or handle. It is a powerful tool, but it can be easily misunderstood, so use caution in where you take it, especially the airport or "concealed" on your person.

Chalice

A cup of any metal, stone, clay, crystal or glass. Silver is popular as it is a Goddess metal, but glass will certainly do. Wine glass or traditional goblet shape is best as the Chalice represents a womb or the Goddess herself, as well as Water and the West Quarter of the Circle. It is important to cleanse and consecrate *one* Chalice and use it always, not a different, random wineglass for every ritual! This is something that can be easily found at a flea market, garage sale, thrift store, etc. I like blue glass as I collect it and the colour blue is associated with the West, but you could certainly also buy an elaborate, fancy Chalice that was made especially for that purpose.

The athame may be dunked into it to represent sex or the joining of male and female energies. The water within it may be stirred deosil to raise energy or widdershins for banishing. Water from the Chalice is sprinkled over items to cleanse and/or empower them. It can be used in fertility magick as it represents the womb (but the cauldron, which also represents the womb is more commonly used) Ritual drink such as the wine in the cakes and wine ceremony may be served in it, but usually it sits in the West during the circle representing the Water element and the Western Quarter. Spring water is best for use in the Chalice, but bottle or tap will do.

Incense and Censor

The Censor can be a regular wooden or metal ash catcher for stick incense, or a small metal or ceramic burner for cone incense, as well as the swinging type on chains that is used by the Catholic Church. This type is good for walking around the circle, but you may prefer a stationary type of censor for your altar or to sit in the Eastern Quarter. Incense represents East, Air, and Yellow. It is a masculine energy and can also be used to represent Spirit, the Fifth Element. It floats up skyward, carrying your message to the God and Goddess and the universe. It cleanses and purifies you, your Circle, and your objects. It is also used to cleanse and consecrate tools and objects and/or empower them. There are hundreds varieties of incense, pure kinds which contain just one ingredient such as jasmine, or blended types which contain several and often have names such as "Love blend" These are widely available over the Internet as well is in many stores. I tend to prefer to use incenses that are of one ingredient to be sure I know what I am using, but there is nothing wrong with utilizing a reputable witch supply websites' blends. Some people make their own incense, which is no doubt most powerful, as is anything made by your own hand.

Incense is a fantastic spell-booster. Even when no incense is called for in a spell it is a good idea to intuit a suitable kind and use it anyway. You will also want to use it help you evoke the Eastern Quarter when you cast your Circle. Staring into the smoke can help produce a trance-like state and allow you to see things in the Spirit realm. Sometimes shapes or stories can be seen in the smoke. Objects are passed through the smoke to cleanse and consecrate as well as empower them. A bowl of sand can be used as a censor in a pinch. As the incense burns down your intent is carried with it. It is a good idea to keep incense going while in the Circle and to light a new stick or cone before the last one is through, as well as to let the Circle incense burn down completely. If you are doing a spell which takes multiple days to complete it is perfectly fine to extinguish and re-light the same stick or cone. Please see *A Witch's Spell Correspondences* for different types of incense and their uses.

Candles

Arguably the most important of all the tools, candles can be utilized for all types of magick. Candles represent the South, Fire, Red. All kinds are good, even inexpensive dollar-store ones, but the best are ones you make yourself or pure, hand poured ones of good quality wax. I used to make candles with homemade moulds. These can be made out of plastic yogurt or soda containers, or even ice cream tubs. Cut off the top (if using a soda or pop bottle) and pierce a hole in the bottom. Thread a length of wick (available at craft stores and online) through the hole and seal it with duct tape. Play out the wick to the new top of the container and tie around a stick which rests across the top and prevents the wick from being lost. Now carefully melt the wax of peeled crayons, old candles (with the wicks removed!) or purchased wax blocks using a lighted taper. You can make a layer candle easily by allowing layers of wax to cool for an hour or so before starting on a new colour. You can add small stones or charms. In my family tradition it is common to make a large marriage candle together with one's spouse, layering the colours according to their uses and adding stones such as rose quartz, and a small coin so that money never drives you apart. This candle is then keep wrapped in dark or red cloth under the marriage bed and lit during wedding anniversaries, when you are trying to get pregnant, when there is strife in the marriage and during spells to strengthen your bond, although it is important to keep it for as long as possible and not throw away the stub even when it can no longer be burned.

There are, of course, other methods for making your own candles, but I have found this to be the safest as well as the most spiritual, as it takes times and forces you to concentrate. It goes without saying that you should be very careful with hot wax as it can cause painful burns and is a bugger to get out of clothes and carpets.

Beeswax candles are good to use because they are natural. Candles are a Masculine energy and sit at the Southern Quarter during the Circle. Candles can be used too at all four Quarters, green in the north, blue in the west, red in the south and yellow in the east, as well as purple in the centre or on the altar for Spirit. You may also use all black candles, or all white, or just one red candle in the South. Some use a white candle to represent the Goddess and a black one for the God or the reverse on the altar. Ideally, candles should be anointed with a suitable oil, such as pine for prosperity, before use. This is done by rubbing a thin layer of oil up from the centre of the candle toward the wick and down from the centre toward the base. A little goes a long way, be careful not to get any dollops of oil near the wick as it is highly flammable. As you will read in the chapter dedicated to colour, different colours of candle can lend different energies to your spell work and they are another powerful spell booster. The candle has been in use for over 5000 years and is an inexpensive and accessible form of correspondence we can use in every spell and Circle. White, red and black candles can be used to represent the Triple aspect of the Goddess, as can green, blue and purple for the Triple God. Candles can represent a person, thing or energy. As the candle burns so does your spell work. Scented candles can be good or bad, depending on the scent. If it's a horrid, overpowering, perfume then it's no good, but a nice, natural essential oil it can be beneficial. Sometimes you can find or make shaped candles that you can work into your spell such as hearts for love magick. They are used to cleanse and consecrate items and tools as well as empower them and direct energy. Objects can be quickly passed through the flames.

NOTE: Candles should not be blown out unless you are banishing something as this blows the energy away! Pinching works, as does a snuffer. Candles can also be extinguished with a sharp hand clap directly above the flame, which causes a down draft. It may take a few tries to perfect this, but it makes an impressive trick when you master it.

Bowl of Salt

Any small dish will do, china, ceramic, metal, clay or terracotta are all ideal. Sea salt is preferable as salt mines are not pleasant places and you don't want to bring that negativity to your magick. The bowl of salt represents North, Green, Earth, and is a feminine energy. It is used to cleanse, consecrate and empower items or tools, and is sprinkled around the Circle during casting, and over items with Chalice water. Small items such as crystals can be left in an empowered bowl of salt in the light of the moon overnight or for seven nights running to cleanse them before use. The salt in the bowl should be changed once a moon or as soon as it gets soiled or "chunky" from getting damp. When you are finished with it empowered salt should be poured out outside or into a body of water if possible.

Pentagram or Pentacle (Altar tile)

A pentagram or pentacle is a representation of the witch's five pointed star in metal, wood, clay or glass. Usually about 3-5 inches in diameter, a Pentagram shows the star encircled while a Pentacle is the star alone. It represents Spirit in the Circle and on the altar. It can also be hung over doors and windows to protect from negative energies and forces. It is worn as a pendant for the same reason or to identify yourself to other witches. It brings luck and money and it is a very old and powerful symbol. It can also represent a human body. An invoking pentagram is drawn starting at the bottom left, then continuing clockwise, a banishing pentagram is opposite. These can be inscribed on candles to aid spell work or in books, on personal items or the back of photographs to protect, push away, or draw in something or someone. It is drawn in the air with wand, athame, or finger in the banishing form to banish or protect, and in the invoking direction to create or strengthen.

Terrible people who consider themselves "devil worshippers" have adopted the inverted pentagram as their sign. This is very annoying as lay people tend not to notice the difference and it casts the Craft, once again, in a negative light. The actual meaning of the inverted pentagram is to draw inwards.

Wand

The wand is a powerful tool long associated with witches and wizards. It is usually a straight length of wood about 18 inches long. Lately metal wands have come into fashion, and there is nothing wrong with them except that if you use metal you miss out on the inherent energies found in the wood. Willow, oak, maple and birch are all good choices, although "birch rod" has some bad connotations. Some people add a crystal or other stone to the tip which is perfectly all right and is quite pleasing to the eye. Some wands are shaped like phalluses. The wand has a masculine energy and is associated with the God and sometimes with the element of Air. It is often used to cast the Circle, raise and direct energy. It is used to describe pentagrams or other magick symbols in the air during spell work. Some people peel the bark off, which I prefer and some leave it on. It can be of any wood, really, as long as you take the time to find one that works for you. It is better not to cut a wand from a living tree, and if you must, take the time to explain your need and be thankful.

It should be cleansed and consecrated before use. Remember it could take many years to find the right wand. I really think this is a tool that it's preferable to find in nature, but you could order one from a witchcraft supply company or buy one from a New Age shop if you are lucky enough to have one in your town. A wand is not "interchangeable" with an athame, but they do serve many of the same functions, so you may wish to have one or the other or both. The wand is waved deosil (clockwise) to raise Power or energy and widdershins (counter-clockwise) to diminish or banish. During the Circle or your spell work you can direct your magick toward your intention by pointing your wand and visualizing the energy pouring through you and out from its tip.

Altar

The altar may be as elaborate or as simple as you choose or have room for. Some witches have huge, beautiful and highly decorative altars permanently set up in their living rooms and others have a special board they place in the Circle. An altar could be of stone (a lovely, if expensive choice) wood, even metal. Your altar could be a special table or your mantle piece. Just remember, you will want to be able to set it up in your Circle and before you when you work your magick. When not in use it could be all packed away or it could have the Chalice, incense censor, South candle, and bowl of salt on it, as well as other meaningful and special magick items such as crystals. Commonly during the Circle an altar will have a representation of the Goddess and God on it, such as a white and black candle, as well as a pentagram, your tools, such as your athame (with the Quarter Representations in their four directions around the Circle) and anything you need for the spell you are going to perform, as well as the cakes and wine for grounding. With that in mind you will want an altar that is big enough for all of this but small enough to be put away unless you are going to have it always on display. Do not use anything with a lid, such as the inside of a trunk, although the top of a trunk would be a good choice, and don't use something such as a book shelf with shelves above it. Remember to try not to use the altar for ordinary tasks in between rituals unless you cleanse and consecrate it each time.

Other Tools:

Besom or Broom

Another item long associated with witches. A magick broom, sometimes called a besom is used to dispel negative energy, either within the Circle or in and around the home. Dancing astride a magick broom is often done at Sabbats. You may wish to find a special old-fashioned twig broom to use for magick. I wouldn't suggest using a plastic broom. Wiccans today hold hands and jump over a broom when getting married and this tradition has been around for many a year. A very base spell involves sweeping vigorously while focusing on banishing or chasing something away.

Cords or Ribbons

Usually they are in a length that is some denomination of 9, such as 27 inches. White, red and black can be braided to represent the Triple aspect of the Goddess, (Maiden, Mother, Crone) likewise with green, blue and purple to represent the Triple aspect of the God (Son, Squire, Sage). Cords or ribbons are used in knot work, and to bind something or someone either to you or away from you. Different colours, like candles have different energies and are used in different types of spells. Another use for cords is to tie them around a limb and restrict blood flow to raise energy and power. This must be done very carefully as if it is done too tightly is can cause numbing or worse. You may or may not wish to attempt this, it is certainly not essential, but is an interesting way of raising energy.

Staffs

Some folk use empowered wooden walking staffs in addition to, or instead of wands. Try to choose the wood according to its property, such as willow or blackthorn for Spirituality. Once again, try to avoid cutting a walking stick from a living tree. One may just find you! It should be cleansed and consecrated before use.

Cauldron

Yet another witchy symbol! Generally three-legged to represent the Goddess' Triple aspect. Used to mix together spell ingredients or blend oils, or sometimes for small bale fires. Incense can be burned inside it, or it can be filled with water and gazed into to attempt to see visions. The cauldron is traditionally used in fertility magick. Stir the cauldron deosil to raise energy or widdershins to banish. Cast iron is a popular choice and can often be found at garage sales or antique stores and the like. The cauldron need not be huge, and can be displayed in the home when not in use, holding pot pourri perhaps. Remember to cleanse and consecrate before use.

Boxes and Bottles

Wooden boxes or glass bottles with stoppers can be used to store stones, herbs, tarot cards and so on once they have been cleansed. All the items for one spell can be sealed inside a box with a tight fitting lid or a bottle with a stopper using the appropriate colour of wax and buried, or tossed into a moving body of water to send the power out, or simply kept out of sight so the items inside continue working together for as long as it takes for the desired result to be achieved. The items can be removed and buried when the spell has worked and run its course.

Poppets and Pouches

These can be made by hand out of a natural fabric such as cotton or leather. Poppets generally represent a person, such as someone you are trying to heal, and are stuffed with herbs, talc, and/or cotton batting or balls. If a poppet represents a specific person you could add (with their permission) finger nail or hair clippings or a photograph of them to focus the magick. Pouches are in themselves spells and might be stuffed with all manner of things: photos, coins, herbs, wax, magick symbols, etc.- depending on their purpose during the Circle and sewn up to complete the spell.

A Grimoire or Book of Shadows

This is where you make a record of your own rituals, spells, and recipes, as well as performing written spells. It traditionally has a black leather cover, but there are many other beautiful types out there. Any special notebook will suffice. You can inscribe it with magickal symbols and protective spells. Usually it is not shown to anyone except those that know about your magickal side and those that you trust completely. It is useful to note the time of day, the phase and sign of the moon and the day of the week that each spell or ritual was preformed and how effective they were. That way, you can begin to notice patterns and choose the best times for your magickal workings. You might also write down dreams, powerful thoughts and ideas, and the results of divination or meditation sessions, as well as knowledge you have gathered about the deities and correspondences.

Some folk use a bell in the Circle for energy raising. A drum or bodhran is great for this too. A white handled knife or bolline can be cleansed and consecrated for use in earthly matters such as herb gathering instead of the athame.

Some folk like to have special jewellery which they wear during all spell work and at the Sabbats. This might be a necklace, bracelet or even a crown. It can be cleansed and empowered and is usually worn only during magickal workings. This magick jewellery might be made with stones that correspond to the energies you are working, such a rose quartz pendent for love spells. It is important to note however, that it is a good idea to remove rings when doing spells as they bind power in your hands and impede the creation and release of energy. I remove mine and keep them on the altar while I work.

In addition a witch may use a variety of tools to divine or predict the future, but I will get into these in *A Witch Divines*.

Notes on Tools:

As much as possible magickal tools should be fashioned by hand or at least handled as much as possible. Plastics and other unnatural materials should not be used in ritual tools. Tools could go under your pillow at night to absorb more of your energy, and can rest in a bowl of salt in the moon's light for seven nights before cleansing and consecrating. Magickal tools should be cleansed and consecrated before use to remove any negativity they might have absorbed and to dedicate them to your magickal work. It is my belief that it is not necessary to cast a Circle for this unless you are doing a bunch of Tools at once.

On a Wednesday or Saturday evening, in spring, if at all possible, purify yourself as discussed in *A Witch's Body of Ritual* or wash your face and hands thoroughly. Sit cross-legged in a quiet place where you will not be disturbed, preferably, as always, outside. Deep breathe for as long as it takes to become calm and focused. Then the tool should be sprinkled with salt and Chalice water, passed through the smoke of a purifying incense (Sage is great) and quickly passed through a white candles' flame. It should be held up to the four directions and straight up to Spirit and then placed on the altar or the ground with your palms pressed flat on it. Imagine your energy pouring into it, filling it with magickal power. Hold it aloft and respectfully ask the Goddess and God to bless it for your magickal use in your own words. You might say something like "Oh Lord and Lady of the Night, please bless this Blank with your favour and Power, so that I may use it for my magickal workings bathed in your Light," Thank them for their attendance by saying something like "My Lady and Lord, I thank you for being here and lending me your Energies on this night, depart with my love". If you do not wish to include the deities at your tool dedication you might simply concentrate on further imbuing the tool with your magickal intent, holding the tool tightly and saying something like "This Blank is dedicated to the magickal work of this witch!"

Now your tool is ready for magickal use!

4: A WITCH'S WHEEL OF THE YEAR

Everything in life goes through cycles and perhaps the most obvious of these cycles is the solar year. The turning of the Wheel of the Year is celebrated in my family's witchcraft with the Greater and Lesser Sabbats or the Sabbats and Esbats.

The Sabbats are best preformed outside, often with the lighting of a balefire in one of the four quarters, and the Circle being cast, but this is not always possible or practical. The Sabbats could be preformed indoors, as I have often found necessary, with a bank of lighted candles standing in for the balefire and sometimes no Circle. The most important thing is to get in touch with the essence of each particular festival, feel the focus of it and be in tune with the cycle of the season. The Sabbats are also a great time for celebrating with friends, and these friends may not be magickal, or indeed, may adhere firmly to other creeds. This does not mean you can't include them! I simply do my ritual celebrating before the guests arrive or after they depart. For Litha I tell them we're having a Solstice Party. Ostara usually falls close to Easter, I generally have people over on Easter weekend (even if

I do my ritual work on the actual equinox) and let people assume they are coming to an Easter party. The same goes for Yule and Samhain, they are assumed to be Christmas and Hallowe'en parties. As a solitary with only some family members and trusted friends "in" on my magickal ways, I find this works best. After all, it's no fun to feast and game alone!

As much as possible feast foods, drink, and decorations should be seasonal and local. There is no point in having fall flowers at Imbolc or strawberries flown in from Goddess knows where at Yule. These are celebrations of the different seasons and times of year and that should be reflected in the food and foliage. I have provided some suggestions below, but you more than anyone will know what is seasonal in your area during the Sabbats. If you are not sure, ask. Most greengrocers, florists, butchers, and the like are happy to talk to customers and explain what is freshest now, even in big chain grocery stores.

Samhain
(Pronounced Sa-*ween*)
October 31 (Also known as Hallowe'en or All Hallows Eve)

This is a Greater Sabbat as well as an ancient Fire Festival, and represents the death of the God and the end of summer. The word Samhain literally means 'summer's end' in the Gaelic. This is also the witch's New Year, although for practical purposes most of us keep to January 1. Modern Hallowe'en springs from Samhain, and all the ghostly, gobliny imagery comes from a perhaps almost instinctual knowledge that this is the time of year when the veil between this world and the next is at its very thinnest (not to mention all the witchy and black cat imagery, which has trickled down over the centuries from times when this was one of the witch's public celebrations).

This is a time for honouring the dead, for divining the future, for letting go of things and people no longer needed. A time to communicate with ancestors, and perhaps ask for their guidance. If at all possible it is best to celebrate this one outside and light the balefire, as well as Cast a Circle.

The balefire should be lit in the Western quarter of the Circle. Decorations could include pumpkins, fall foliage, pomegranates or other seasonal fruits, and definitely apples. Why not include a jack-o-lantern in your Circle? After all, they were originally made by pagans to chase away negativity and mischievous spirits. Colours for Samhain are orange, black and red. Activities in the Circle include scying in the smoke of the balefire and honouring the dead by listening to their favourite music and looking at photographs. You may also wish to consider telling your dearly departed that you are doing okay and they may rest easy. Another good thing to do is write down the things you wish to be rid of and throw the list into the fire (or carefully burn it in a candle's flame) while visualizing these things gone from your life. This is the end of an old year and the beginning of a new one. A time for a fresh start. A time to rid oneself of negativity. For a full celebration:

Decorate your celebratory area

Purify yourself (as discussed in Chapter 5: *A Witch's Body of Ritual*)

Cast the Circle (as discussed in Chapter 11).

Scry in the smoke or in a vessel of water (as discussed in *A Witch Divines*).

Call to the departed, remembering to honour them, perhaps with their favourite music, and let them know you are doing well and they may be at peace.

Dance around the fire bidding the God (and your loved ones) farewell. He is gone until the spring, or the next cycle, but we know he will return, just as we know we will meet our departed loved ones again.

Focus on endings, dissolving of partnerships that no longer

work, changing things and perhaps giving them a new incarnation, and the culmination of projects, as well as feeling close to those that are no longer with us. Write down (and burn) anything you wish to be rid of.

Thank the Goddess and the departing God.

Close the Circle and ground (as discussed in Chapter 5)

When you go back inside leave offerings out for the Goddess (and the animals), traditionally this would include several apples cut across the middle to reveal the pentagram within. If you are working indoors try to leave some apples at a nearby park, or make a donation to a local food bank.

Now you can tidy away your ritual things and invite family and friends to join you for a large feast! Foods could include dishes made from pumpkins and apples, as well as potatoes, cheeses, sausages and other pork dishes and nuts. Perhaps pumpkin or apple pie for dessert. Ale is a good traditional drink for Samhain. This should be a big feast to enjoy the last of the fresh meats and vegetables before winter sets in (obviously you will still be eating fresh foods over the winter, but try to imagine yourself back in the times when this would be the last big meal of fresh stuffs for awhile). Games like bobbing for apples are very classical, and this is a great time to build a "haunted house" or help youngsters with their costumes. Most Hallowe'en activities are perfect for Samhain fun. You could also honour the dead by setting a place for them at your table or visiting their graves at this time.

Yule
December 21 (or whichever day the Solstice falls on)

This is a lesser Sabbat or Esbat, and represents renewal and the promise of spring's return. The God is not with us, but the Goddess carries new life within her. It also represents the death of the Holly King (winter) and the rise of the Oak King (summer). In a large coven, two male witches will act this out. This is the time of year when we remind our self that spring will indeed return, often by bringing green branches into the home. We have evidence that spring will come again as the days begin to get longer after this. This is a much older festival than Christmas! It was adopted as the birth of Christ to help ease the conversion of pagans to Christianity by allowing them to keep one of their most important festivals. The birth of Christ could be seen as a parallel to the re-birth of the Sun.

If you can work outside a balefire may be lit in the Southern quarter of the Circle. Why not also have a Christmas tree at this time? They serve the purpose of this festival nicely by reminding us that spring and green things will return. You could certainly have fun searching for decorations with a witchy theme, or simply using lights, balls, and of course, five-pointed stars! Other decorations could include fires, wheel symbols such as wreaths, holly branches, snowdrops and ivy, as well as the colours red and green and silver. This is a time for acknowledging the turning of the Wheel of the Year.

For a full ritual:
Decorate your space and purify yourself.
Light the balefire to the South.
Cast the Circle.
Visualize the death of the Holly King and imagine the rise of the Oak King, perhaps wearing a crown of holly leaves at the start of the ritual and switching to a crown of oak leaves at the middle, if you can get them.

The Great Rite may take place now (see *A Witch's Sex Magick*).

Meditate, or perhaps recite a poem or song about the Turning of the Wheel of the Year and the sun's return.

Focus on the idea of what goes around comes around, that all things return, the sun, the spring, even our own souls.

Honour the Goddess and the hope of the God's return.

Close the Circle and ground (as discussed in Chapter 5).

Now is a great time for a "Christmas" party, or you may wish to call it a holiday party. Foods might include preserves, roast pork, goose or hen, nuts and dried fruits, as well as potatoes and turnips. Plus, or course, desserts such as short bread, gingerbread, fruit cake and plum pudding and wines or stronger spirits to keep out the cold! Why not bake cookies with love for your guests and perhaps a homeless shelter? Another great activity we always do is to make popcorn and cranberry garlands and string them in the trees for the hungry birds, as well as spreading peanut butter on pine cones and hanging them as lovely natural bird feeders. You could give little gifts, maybe homemade, and play games with friends and family. Dance and revel, spring will return!

Imbolc
February 2 (Also known as Imbolg or Candlemas)

This is a Greater Sabbat representing the quickening of the year and the Goddess' womb. It is a festival of lights to encourage spring's return. A crown of candles or lights may be worn. This is very much a Goddess festival. Now is the time to turn away from the inner workings and the inner focus of winter and towards others and the outside world. The Goddess is with child and the promise of spring. This is also a time for blessing and planting seeds. You may wish to light every room in your house for a time before your ritual. Decorations include any flowers that are available such as paper whites, the first crocus and mistletoe. The colour is white. Traditional decorations include a dish of snow and a dish of milk. A crown of lights and a phallus-shaped wand are appropriate. The colours are green, white, and yellow. Candles could be grouped to the north of the Circle in the stead of a balefire. It is traditional to save some of the harvest at Lammas, sometimes in the form of a corn dolly or a bundle of corn shuck and bring it forth now.

For a full ritual:

Purify yourself and decorate your space.

Cast the Circle and walk around clockwise (deosil) with a candle in hand.

Light your bank of candles or balefire to the North of the Circle with the candle.

Kiss the corn dolly and the wand (if using) and place forming an X in the centre of the Circle.

Don the crown of lights (if using) and welcome the pregnant Goddess.

Bless the seed you will be planting this year and plant some while focusing on the themes of the festival: Spring and Goddess quickening, ewe's giving birth, sap rising, the bringing of light to aid the God to return.

Burn or bury the corn shuck (if using).

Focus on fertility magick, creation, beginnings, new ideas, and the returning of light.

The Great Rite may be enacted now.

Honour the Goddess again, perhaps with verse, song or chant.

Close the Circle, Earth the Power.

Leave your bowl of milk outside for the Goddess (and the animals) if possible. Now you may want to do "spring cleaning". This is the traditional time for actual cleaning of your indoor space, as well as blessing and purifying it with a cleansing incense such as pine or sage. Visit every room (even if it doesn't need actual cleaning) smoking it with incense and concentrating on removing any built-up negativity and making it fresh for the coming spring. After this is a time for feasting! If you want to include non-magickal folk you can always tell them you wanted a party to celebrate the retreat of dreary winter or even that you are celebrating ground hog day. This is a fine time for dancing and party games like Truth or Dare. Feast food might include lamb or beef and any young fresh vegetables that are available, as well as blond beers and light desserts such as custards or angel food cakes.

Ostara
March 21, or whichever day the Spring Equinox falls on.

(Also known as Eostre, which leads us obviously to Easter. This is another pagan festival which predates and was "borrowed" by Christianity as we can clearly see in its mythology of re-birth).

This is a lesser Sabbat or Esbat, preformed when the day and night are of equal length. It represents the official coming of spring and the birth of the God! He has returned to us and this is a great time to celebrate and perform the Great Rite. You may wish to make "Ostara eggs" and empower them with love and harmony. This is the traditional time to review your magick supply cupboard as well as your tools and see what is needed as well as purchase, look for, or make new items. Decorations include wheels, eggs, a large bouquet of daffodils and other seasonal flowers, spring branches (cut with thanks and love), a plant potted at Imbolc and the colours white and green.

For a full Ritual:
Decorate your Ritual Space and purify yourself.
Cast the Circle.
Dance around it astride a broom, full of joy!
Light a balefire (or bank of candles) in the Eastern Quarter, (inside the Circle this time).
Honour the Goddess and the newly-born God. You may wish to sing, chant or read a verse about birth and new life.
Walk deosil around the Circle with the flowers in hand.
Sit and focus on what you would like to manifest in the coming season, perhaps holding onto the pot of seedlings planted at Imbolc.

Focus on the themes of this time: growing, newness, the seedlings of ideas and projects, what you would like to achieve during the year between now and the next Ostara.

The Great Rite should be enacted or preformed for real now (see *A Witch's Sex Magick*).

Thank the Goddess and the infant God for their blessings and attendance.

Close the Circle and ground.

If you are having guests over for an "Easter party" lamb is the perfect thing to serve them, perhaps with new potatoes and spring onions roasted in the pan, spinach or some other fresh green vegetables and puddings and fresh fruit for dessert, perhaps with a light, sweet white wine. You could have an egg hunt for the young ones, and of course there is nothing wrong with enjoying some chocolate eggs!

Beltane

May 1 (Also known as May Day, Beltaine, Bealtuinn).

This is a Greater Sabbat as well as an ancient Fire festival and is thought to be one of the oldest holidays or festivals in the world. It represents the recovery of the Goddess and the growth of the God. It is a time for chasing away the last winter cobwebs, settling debts, dedicating new tools and marking the true end of winter. It is the return of fertility, and another time the Great Rite is important. The God is becoming a mature consort for the Goddess and they are exploring each other sexually.

Decorations include seasonal flowers such as hyacinths, lilac branches (cut with love and thanks), young oak leaves and hawthorn branches, as well as ribbons and mirrors, and if possible a May pole. This is an upright pole with two balls hanging from it. One is silver and one gold. They represent the sun and the moon as well as testicles. The pole has long pink and blue ribbons hanging from it which are entwined in opposite directions by boys and girls. This may not be at all possible for you to do, but if it is you could have youngsters do the May pole dance when you have guests over for feasting after your ritual. The colours are yellow and white.

For a full Ritual:

Decorate your space, including erecting a May pole to the East of the Circle, if possible.

Purify yourself.

Cast the Circle.

Dance and raise energy deosil around the Circle.

If you have a Maypole use your athame to cut a door in the Circle and then dance around the Maypole, entwining the ribbons (they can be unentwined later for any children to re-do it. This may be impossible if you are a solitary, and that is alright).

Return to and seal the Circle. Celebrate the God's Growth and His and the Goddess' new found love.

Focus on the themes of this festival: Love, romance, fertility.

Scry in the mirror.

Athames may be plunged into Chalices or Swords into Cauldrons.

The Great Rite should happen now!

Dedicate any new tools to the Goddess and God's favour.

Thank the Goddess and her Consort

Close the Circle and ground.

Bless your garden or your potted plants or a garden at a park and visualize them growing with abundance and beauty.

Celebrate with a big feast. This is one of a witch's most important festivals. Spring has sprung! Feast your guests with chicken or beef cooked with lots of fresh herbs and vegetables. Have ice cream for dessert perhaps, and lots of beers and wines.

Litha

June 21, or the actual day of the Solstice.

This is a lesser Sabbat or an Esbat and represents the joining or mating of the Goddess and God and the conception of the new God. On this longest day of the year the Oak King and Holly King once again do battle and the Oak King falls. Summer is here and the Goddess and God are mature, powerful and very much together. My favourite of all the festivals, except perhaps Samhain. This is a time of Great Magickal Power. You may wish to do your ritual at dawn (and go back to bed to be rested for the feasting later). This is a great time to work love or partnership magick, as well as an excellent day to gather herbs.

The colours are white, blue and pink. Decorations include a cauldron with flowers floating in it or ringed with flowers, the Circle formed with stones, heather, oak leaves, and many pink and blue flowers and candles.

For a full Ritual:

Purify yourself and decorate your ritual space.

Light the balefire (or bank of candles) to the south.

Cast the Circle.

Drums may be beaten to raise energy.

Visualize the Oak King thrown down by the Holly King.

Focus on the theme that there can be no light without darkness, as well as the themes of love, maturity, and partnerships.

Collected herbs are blessed and prepared for drying.

Leap the balefire.

Dance and revel, it is summertime!

Work love magick for yourself or others.

Once again, athames and swords are plunged into Chalices and Cauldrons.

The Great Rite should happen now!

Honour the joining of the Goddess and God and thank them.

Close the Circle and ground.

The days are long and warm, the Goddess and God are at full strength. This is a wonderful time for working magick of all kinds. There should be a large feast with friends and relatives and much celebrating. The house should be filled with flowers and candles. This is a great time for a barbecue as well. Why not have a buffet style dinner with lots of salads, burgers and kabobs with a big cake for dessert and plenty of beer and coolers? Your guests will love it and they are bound to be filled with joy and amorous leanings even if they don't quite know why! Be sure to toast the moon! Summer is here!

Lammas

August 1 (Also known as Lughnasdh).

This is a Greater Sabbat or Esbat and represents the first harvest and the celebration of the God as he first begins to diminish. We are thankful for the bounty of the season and our many blessings. Why not try your hand at baking loaves, muffins, pretzels etc. and donate some of your efforts to a food bank?

Decorations include corn shucks, sometimes fashioned into corn dollies, grains, loaves of bread, lilies, poppies and peaches. The colours are red and orange.

For a full Ritual:

Decorate your space with the bounty of the season.

Purify yourself.

A balefire or bank of candles may be lit to the East of the Circle.

Cast the Circle.

Dance around the Circle.

Focus on being thankful for all you have and what you are proud of, as well as Honouring the God and Goddess.

Fashion a dolly out of corn shuck for next Imbolc (optional).

A witch (usually male, but if you are a solitary female it is fine to do this yourself) dances anti-clockwise (widdershins) around the Circle as the God is diminishing.

Thank the Goddess and the Diminishing God.

Close the Circle and Earth the Power.

Feasting and games should follow. Specially baked muffins and breads are great to have now. Fish, beef or pork make a fine main course, served with tomatoes and other seasonal vegetables. Peach pies and cobblers make an excellent dessert. Wines and beers should be full bodied and rich. Have the feast outdoors if possible, perhaps as a picnic.

Mabon
September 21, or whichever day the Equinox falls on.

This is a Lesser Sabbat or Esbat and represents the second harvest and the last days of the God. He grows old and tired now. Soon he will be cut down as the harvest. Once again we are thankful for all we have and the Goddess and God's bounty. This is the time to begin turning inward for winter. The introspection and examination of one's life that are at their height at Samhain begin now.

Decorations include pine branches (thankfully and lovingly cut), nuts, pine cones, acorns, corn, and dried leaves. Also, pears, apples and other seasonal fruits. The colours are red and brown. You could press leaves now to give as Yule gifts. The God is an old man now.

For a full Ritual:
Decorate your space,

Purify yourself,

Cast the Circle,

In a large coven a dance with kisses on the cheek is performed. If you are a solitary you may dance alone.

Focus on the balance of light and dark, as well as inner life, perhaps on what you would like to improve about your character or mental state.

Fruit is blessed. It is proof of the God and Goddess' love!

Toss leaves into the air.

Reflect on the joys of your life and your blessings.

The Great Rite may take place now.

Eat apples and other fruit and thank the Goddess and the old God.

Close the Circle and ground.

Games with piles of leaves may take place with family and friends tonight. Serve a feast that includes wheat, corn, pork or beef, as well as lots of baked goods and fruits. A dark beer is appropriate now. There is a feeling of abundance and prosperity now. Celebrate!

Over the seasons you may develop and incorporate you own myths and celebrations into the festivals. No two celebrations will be exactly alike. Consider what each time of the cycle means to you and what is freshest in your area. There is no right or wrong way to observe the Sabbats, as long as you are in touch with the feeling and essence of each one.

5: A WITCH'S BODY OF RITUAL

There are, of course, a million rituals written in books of all kinds dating from ancient times to last week, and you will create new ones all the time. No two will ever be exactly the same. But each one does, and generally should, follow the same basic format. This is part of what makes it ritual. A lot of the power of ritual comes from doing the same actions over and over and in the same ways to prepare the mind for the work. The basic format for a witch's ritual is:

Preparing yourself, physically and magickally.

Preparing the space you'll be using, physically and magickally

Creating your magickal space (for some this is known as creating sacred space) and/or Casting the Circle (sometimes called Invocation).

Observing the Sabbats (on Sabbats, obviously).

Energy raising (for spells) and spell work.

Saying thank you and farewell to the Lady and Lord and/or the Elementals.

Closing the Circle.

Grounding or Earthing the Power.

To prepare yourself for magickal workings and observances it is a good idea to use some form of purification or cleansing. This usually consists of a ritual bath taken with herbs such as sage or lavender, or a little salt. Depending on any spell work you may be about to do you may wish to add other herbs, like rose petals or jasmine flowers if love work is on the agenda. A ritual bath can be very quick, just a dunk in and out, or as long as you like. Sometimes a good soak in scented water helps to prepare you for the magickal workings. In extreme cases, such as when you are in a hurry, the hands and face may be washed only. Preparing yourself for working magick also includes meditation and deep breathing. Meditation is a many layered process that may take years to perfect. If you are unfamiliar with meditation simply start out by sitting comfortably with a straight spine and closing your eyes. Breathe slowly and deeply, inhaling through your nose and exhaling through your mouth. Picture something like a calm blue ocean, an orange sunset, your favourite garden, or anything that relaxes you. You may choose to repeat a phrase or syllable such as the familiar "Om." The difficult part is thinking of, well nothing. The key is to empty your mind, work on your focus and remove yourself from the everyday, as well as cleanse yourself of negativity, worries, and anxiety. This is vital for the working of magick. If you still feel everyday problems or issues intruding you can also try standing in a bracing wind and concentrating on feeling all the built up negative energy leaving you, or drumming in a soft rhythm, imagining that with each pound of the instrument you are cleaner, purer, and free of the mundane and the things that bog you down. At this time you can also anoint your body with an oil appropriate to the magick working you will be doing, such as Patchouli for protection, (see *A Witch's Correspondences*). Use a drop on your forehead or "third eye," your throat, the centre of your chest, on or above your genitals and on the top of each foot (needless to say you should skin test all oils 48 hours beforehand by dabbing the oil undiluted on a small patch of the sensitive skin on the inside of your upper arm. Essential oils can be very irritating and may need to be diluted in a "carrier oil" such as almond). Dress in special clothing of a natural material.

When preparing your space, whether you consider the natural world sacred already (as Celts often do,.) or you want to make it sacred for your workings, a lot of cleansing is usually not necessary if the ritual is preformed outside, which is generally better although it is certainly not always possible to work outside, and indoor work can be just as effective). A light sweep with a besom or magick broom and a little sprinkling of salt and water will usually suffice, especially if you can find a spot that is out of the way of human traffic. However, if the ritual is to be done indoors, some cleansing is a good idea. Start by unplugging the telephone and turning any cell phones 'Off.' Try to make sure you will not be otherwise disturbed. This may be difficult! It may be necessary to perform your ritual late at night or early in the morning. You don't want a child or partner bursting into your Circle if it can be avoided. That being said, it is not 'The End of the World' if your Circle is interrupted. After you have kindly asked anyone who has wandered in to take a hike you can repair the Circle with your athame, wand, or pointer finger and go on with your magick work, or close the Circle, thank the deities, ground yourself and begin again at another time. If you are interrupted in such a way that you cannot do these things, try to eat or drink something to ground yourself and say at least a quick thanks to the Lord and Lady. They will understand if you have to do this properly later. You must try to always close the Circle. The one exception to the 'no interruptions' plan could be an animal. A cat or dog may be a welcome addition to your spell, ritual, or Sabbat observance, but this depends largely on the animal. You don't want a dog who knocks over candles with an enthusiastic tail, or a cat who "attacks" cords, so you may want to shut them away. The indoor area should be swept, and if there's been fighting or upset in the house, or visitors who make you uncomfortable it should be mopped or vacuumed. While you do this, and when you make a final pass over with your magick broom visualize sparks of white or blue light shooting out from broom's bristles and chasing away negativity. A vacuum could be seen as literally sucking up negativity and discord so it can be thrown away. You may also wish to carry a purifying type of incense such as sage, thyme, rosemary, or frankincense around the room and sprinkle salt and water about.

Creating your magickal working space is mainly about casting the Circle, which we will get into in further detail In *A Witch's Circle*. This also includes setting up your altar, either in the centre of the Circle or to the North or East. As much as I would love to have a permanent altar set up, it is not feasible in the home I am in, and this may also be the case in your home, so now is the time to arrange all your ritual tools on a suitable surface, as well as any Sabbat items or spell correspondences you may be using. This is also a good time to mark with chalk, the tip of a magick sword or regular knife, salt, or a specially measured cord or rope the boundaries of the Circle. Stones or powdered herbs mixed in with salt will work nicely as well. Then the Circle is cast (see *A Witch's Circle*). Invocation, a term used in many Circle castings is a powerful, even dangerous thing. You must never ever, *ever* Invoke or summon something you don't understand, or haven't taken the time to research even with proper precautions. That being said, we like to ask the deities to be present and this is the time to respectfully request the presence of the Lady and Lord to witness your ritual and aid in your magickal work. This is usually done with a spoken verse or prayer, chanting, drumming, or the ringing of bells. Rhyme is very useful at this time. It needn't be "word perfect" or even the same every time. It serves the dual purpose of requesting the deities presence and waking the power within you. All of the actions leading up to a ritual help to create and reinforce the magick. You are setting your mind the way a stage is set up to evoke a scene in a play. The repetitiveness of all the preparations helps you get in focus. Some part of your mind will say, "Ahh, we're going to create magick now," as you go through the steps and get ready.

Sabbat observance might include scrying during Samhain or the blessing and planting of seeds during Imbolc. Observances may also include meditation, dancing, revels, and thanksgiving or a few moments spent focusing on the theme or energy of the Sabbat (see *A Witch's Wheel of the Year*).

Energy raising (used for spells) is the root of all magick and spell-work. This where the power comes from that leads to the manifestation of your magickal intent, i.e. the desired outcome of your spell. If you are simply celebrating a Sabbat, doing divination or attempting to commune with a loved one who has passed you may not need to raise energy at all. If you are performing a spell however it is important to create or raise some power and energy to make it work. Energy raising is usually easier during a full moon or Sabbat but these are not always the ideal times for spell work, depending on the sort of magick you want to manifest. During energy raising, power is built up within you and then released and sent toward your goal. There are a variety of ways to create this power or energy, drumming, chanting, dance. I was always taught that the two best ways to raise energy are with sex magick and visualization. A properly cast circle will help keep energy in until you are ready to send it on its way, so don't worry about it seeping away before you are ready to let it go. Once you are ready to send the energy you can direct it outward and it will go right through the Circle (Magick, huh?).

The Great Rite and other forms of sex magick are tremendously powerful. The energy raised by two loving, excited partners who concentrate together on directing that energy toward a magickal goal is almost unmatched. As a solitary, self-stimulation can be used to raise powerful energy. The key in both cases is to focus on directing that energy at the moment of climax toward your magickal intention.

71

Visualization is also an excellent form of energy raising. Aided by the focus provided by the correct correspondences (such as coloured candles, herbs, incense, pictures and oils), the mind can create enough power to truly alter your situation. It is important to focus beforehand with deep breathing and/or relaxation techniques to get yourself into the right place to raise energy, whatever method you will be using. Spend a few moments gathering yourself and thinking about your intent before you begin to chant, drum, dance, visualize, or use sex magick. The intensely charged atmosphere of the Circle helps a lot. You must really *see* the changes taking place. You must *know* that it is going to happen. It is good to be operating under a suspension of disbelief because the instant, the very *instant* a shadow of a doubt creeps in you are in danger of sabotaging your own magick. But when you believe, and know that anything can happen you have within you the power to really change your world (see *A Witch's Sex Magick,* and *A Witch's Spells* for more on how to use sex magick and visualization in your spells).

Some spell work will be done before energy raising and some afterwards. If you are using a talisman, amulet, pouch, or poppet you will want to pour some of the energy into it as well as sending it out into the universe. You may wish to prepare the item first, for example sew up three sides of a pouch, work on creating the energy and then send it into the objects and then the assembled bundle. Other spells will be mostly about raising the energy and sending it out. To help make decisions about the order of events see again *A Witch's Spells.*

Thanking the Lord and Lady (and anybody else you have asked to be present, such as Elementals) is definitely a good idea. This can be done in a number of ways, with verse or chant or even song. Just be respectful and grateful. They've witnessed your ritual and hopefully helped boost your magick, and you hope they will come again.

Grounding (sometimes called Earthing the Power), is also a

very good idea, as your head will be in an unusual place, and you may feel outside of yourself. Although you've sent out your energy toward your magick intent you are still in a power-charged atmosphere. Even if you haven't done a spell there is energy in the Circle that needs to be dissipated. There are several methods for this; the traditional cakes and ale (or cakes and wine) is a good one. Special crescent-shaped cakes are eaten with a cup of beer or wine. Fruit, cheese, or bread and pure fruit juice could be substituted, as long as you are eating and drinking something fairly simple and natural to get your body into a different mode. The blood leaves your head and goes to your stomach to aid in digestion, and this brings your mind back to Earth. You can use a basic sugar cookie recipe, adding some finely ground almonds and shaping the cookies into crescents by hand or using a special crescent shaped cookie cutter. Ground almonds are a traditional addition but you may use other recipes as long as they are fairly plain (no double chocolate crescent cakes please!). In addition to a snack and drink you can press your palms flat onto the ground and picture (and feel) the magick energy running out of you and back into the Earth.

Closing the Circle is discussed in *A Witch's Circle*, but you will now want to pick up any stones or cords you may have used to mark the Circles' boundaries and generally tidy up. Sweep the area clean of salt, chalk, herbs and ashes, and put away your tools and candles. Offerings of cakes and ale (or whatever you've used for grounding) should be left outside in a libation bowl or simply on the ground. You may not always be able to do this where you live. Sometimes, for example I toss my offerings into the woods, bury them or throw them into a body of water. I trust the Lady and Lord understand.

Wearing special clothes for magick is also discussed in *A Witch's Circle*, but it is worth noting that not all of us can afford or easily obtain a special outfit for magick right away. If this is the case, wash something made of natural materials and sprinkle it with salt and water before you wear it for magick. Some people also like to have special magick jewellery that they wear during Circles, Sabbats, spell casting, and rituals such as drawing the moon into you. This is a lovely idea, and the stones or metals in the jewellery can lend their unique energies to your magick. If you want to use magick jewellery cleanse it as you would a magickal tool and keep it somewhere special when not in use. In terms of regular jewellery you can keep it on for magick rituals but try to be aware of any negativity it may have absorbed and remove it or cleanse it beforehand if you think it has any "bad vibes," i.e. you have had an argument or uncomfortable experience while wearing it. It is always a good idea to remove rings when doing magick as they can bind your power and impede its release. The exception might be wearing engagement rings or wedding bands during love magick as their special energies can aid the spell.

6: A WITCH'S GARDEN

In times past witches were sometimes referred to as "herb women" or "hedge wizards" and the art of "wort cunning" is as old as the Craft itself. Herbal healing is an ancient practice and now much of it is being scientifically proven. Herbs lovingly home-grown and hand-cultivated are a marvellous enhancement to cooking, and who does not love a beautiful, colourful flower garden? But both herbs and flowers, as well as fruits, vegetables, shrubs, and trees have magickal uses too. When I was growing up my family's garden included many plants which were used for magickal purposes such as daffodils for love, good luck and raising a wind or rain shower, lilies for love and protection and poppies for pain relief and love. A large bouquet of lilac branches would be brought inside in the spring to restore harmony to the house after it was empty all winter and is grown for protection and attracting faeries. In addition to being used in cooking (especially with lamb), mint is said to ease stomach pain when the leaves are brewed in a tea or eaten raw. Family legend even states that sick animals will come to the garden and eat mint to feel better. Foxglove is for protection and attracting Earth Elementals. Morning glory is for divination, as is dandelion. Geraniums protect a witch's house, especially from strangers with dubious intentions. Peony's roots can be dried and worn as a protective charm and the flowers can be used in a protection spell. I cannot say enough about lavender. Grow it for luck. For love. For headaches, for sore eyes. Bathe in it, include it in headache pillows, in love pouches and soaps. Lavender is great for inducing restful sleep and feelings of calm and peace. It protects against abuse, especially spousal. Creates happiness and promotes long life. It is sacred to the Goddess and can be used in child birth; it is a wonderful smelling and beautiful herb that should be included in every witch's garden. It likes partial to full sun and fast draining soil. Asparagus stirs up bodily lust. Rosemary is protective, particularly when planted at the edges of a garden of property, is good for love magick, and is wonderful in cooking. Bee balm attracts butterflies and Air Elementals, Devil's Paintbrush Fire Elementals although it is often considered a weed. Any water plants can be used to attract Water Elementals, as well as blue hyacinths. Faeries like pansies and roses. Roses are great for love, if somewhat over used. We kept hyacinths also to aid with sadness, heather for rain magick and to honour ancestors, garlic for love. Ficus and money plant are good for prosperity, clover for luck. Jasmine and passionflower work wonders for love and lust, as well as strawberry leaves, flowers, and the fruit itself. Sweet-pea is good for making friends and bravery, thistle for luck and difficult situations. Ferns are used for rain magick. Tulips and trilliums (Ontario's Provincial flower) are both good for love and luck. Iris is for love and the root, also known as orris root, is a powerful aid in love spells. Lily of the Valley is protective and a bouquet of it will make you happy. Sweet woodruff is for prosperity and luck in business. Lemon balm, also called Melissa, is good for headaches and digestive ills, as well as love magick. Gardenia is for love (there is a lot of magick devoted to love!) Violets are for lust and impatiens protect your home and are lucky. Raspberry leaves are good for burns. Cedar trees will try their best to protect those that they live with, and black walnuts are very lucky. Birches have short life spans and are good for prosperity magick, but it may not be long lasting. The mighty oak is sacred to Jack O' the Green and aids with love work and an acorn makes a fine talisman for love or luck....I could go on and on! In *A Witch's Spell Correspondences* I give lists of correspondences for various types of magickal workings such as love, healing, and prosperity. There are many very good books and other resources that list what each flower is "for" and as always, you will know more when you handle each plant yourself.

Some of the plants I have listed, it may be noted, are weeds. That has always been fine among my family. A witch's garden is not usually a regimented, chemical-treated, too-perfect country club. It is a wild, beautiful, free, and oft overgrown place of magick. That is not to say that it cannot be neat, but our gardens were never too severe. It is best to avoid chemicals whenever possible. (in some areas they are banned anyhow). Pesticides are a nasty business. The damage done by DDT alone in North America is just revolting. There are natural products available and hundreds of home remedies (such as sprinkling eggshells about and planting marigolds to keep down slugs) on the Internet and in books. Green witchcraft is just that - green and beneficial to the planet rather than harmful. Toads, ladybugs and spiders, as well as dragonflies and bats can be welcome residents in a witch's garden as they eat "bad bugs" such as aphids and mosquitoes. Nobody wants a bee's nest under their eaves but it is worth remembering that the honey bee population is in decline and without bees the crops we depend on would be no more.

Herbs and vegetables should be planted during a new or waxing moon in Cancer, or Scorpio. Garlic should be planted during a waxing moon in Sagittarius. Sage should be planted during a full moon in any of the water signs. Flowers should be planted, if at all possible, during a waxing moon in the sign of Libra. Certain signs of the moon are more suited to planting and growth; these are Taurus, Cancer, Libra, Scorpio, Capricorn and Pisces. The signs of Aries, Gemini, Leo, Virgo, Sagittarius and Aquarius are considered "barren" or less beneficial. It is always best to plant during a new or waxing moon in a beneficial sign and try never to plant or transplant during a waning moon or a less beneficial sign (except garlic and sage). The weeds you don't want or destructive plants and vines can be destroyed during the waning moon, especially in the signs of Leo, Aquarius and Virgo. Pruning when you wish to discourage further growth can be done at this time also, whereas if you want to encourage growth you should prune during the waxing moon in a beneficial sign, especially Cancer or Taurus. Lunar phases and signs can be found in any good witch's, magickal or farmer's almanac as well as for free online. This lunar knowledge is very old and is generally the basis for "plant" and "harvest" days in farmer's almanacs.

Harvesting plants for drying should be done on a dry day before the sun is at its highest in the sky. It is always a good idea to ask the plant's permission and to thank the plant that you take from. This can be done quietly and in your own words. You might say something like "Little (or great) plant of Blank, please may I clip from you only a little leaf (or twig, flower, etc.) for my need is true." Wait a moment and see if you feel anything. If you feel a strong negative it is best to leave it and come back another time. Once you have clipped, thank the plant. You might say "Little Blank plant I thank you for sharing your abundance with me. I am very grateful." You might feel silly doing this but you don't want your magick to backfire because you didn't take a moment to be thankful. Fresh flowers should be cut towards sunset. Don't water between 11 AM and 2 PM or during the hottest hours of sun. Try, instead, to water during the early morning or around sunset, and don't cut your grass too short. It will need less watering if it is a little longer. If plants start to yellow you may be giving them too much water. You can dry herbs upside down in small bunches. For this my family now uses rubber bands rather than string as the plants sometimes shrink as they dry. Keep them out of the sun and check them after about a week. They should be dry enough to move to baggies, jars or bottles.

Of course I don't even need to mention (but I am) that you must never ever ingest any plant without being totally sure of what it is. Thinking you know is not knowing.

It is said that a witch may keep red flowers in their garden and that they will point their heads toward the direction from which trouble is approaching, but I have never found this to be true. Perhaps this is because I don't like red flowers though, and we never kept many excepting poppies. A rowan tree is said to be a witch's bane, but again I have not found this to be so. Growing your own pumpkins for Samhain is an excellent thing to do if you have the space. They like having a hill for each plant, full sun and fast draining soil, as well as about a bucket of water for each plant each day. If you are living in an apartment you may have only a balcony or a window sill and that is fine as well. You can have quite a nice assortment of small potted herbs and flowers and even a small tree or two even in limited space. Potted plants can be moved in and out of the sun and you can make use of the wonderfully rich potting soil commercially available. Make your selections carefully according to your magickal needs and see how long you can keep your plants living, many years if you care for them. For those that live in the country or have some space around them it is a good idea to get a PH test of your soil to have a better idea what you can best grow as some plants prefer more acidity and some more alkaline soils. Observe your land and see what areas get the most sun, which are most protected from wind, etc before you plant. Some family members like to make a pentagram shape out of bricks or stones and plant different herbs in all the sections. Dried herbs can be used in spells, pouches, poppets, healing or baths. An herbal bath is an excellent way to relax or change your mood. Throw a bunch of dried herbs right into the water with you, or if you prefer, tie up a bundle in cloth such as cotton or cheesecloth and hang them under the tap as the tub fills. Try rosemary for invigoration, lavender for healing and relaxing, jasmine or roses for lover's baths, or sage for aches and pains and purification.

Don't feel silly about talking to your plants, gently running your hands over their leaves, stems and branches, even singing to them. Studies show that plants that are spoken to do better, although they do not have much taste in music.

When starting a new garden or working on a new section of an existing one, or even when planting some potted herbs for a window sill you may want to cast a spell over the plants to ensure fertility and longevity. Do your spell on the day you work on planting after the plants are in the ground. This should be during a new or waxing moon in Taurus, Cancer, Scorpio, Capricorn, Pisces or Libra for flowers. You will need: Two green candles, a brown candle and a blue candle, a small stone or crystal, your wand or athame, your chalice, your watering can, and some pine or basil incense.

Start off by finding a quiet place where you will not be disturbed. Set up the four candles in holders in a square shape in front of you along with a filled chalice, the rock or crystal, and the incense in the holder. Your watering can should be empty and off to the one side. Deep breathe and centre yourself until you are ready to begin.

Now chant softly:
"Flower and herb, stalk and leaf,
Grow tall, strong, and dig deep.
Stretch you roots and feel the earth,
Reach up to the sun.
With love and power the magick's begun."

Light the four candles and the incense. Drop the crystal into the chalice and use your wand or athame to inscribe an invoking pentagram over it. Spend some time visualizing your plants growing strong, tall, and healthy, blooming, or bushing out. Close your eyes and see your garden as you want it to be, all while circling your wand or athame clockwise over the chalice.

Chant softly:

"Taller and stronger with each passing moon,
You grow up for my magick soon.
Drink of these waters, feel the wind blow.
I reap the magick that I sow.
With love and power the magick is done."

Spend a few more minutes stirring the chalice water clockwise with the tip of your wand or athame and envisioning a glorious garden full of healthy green plants. Pour the chalice into the watering can, stone and all, and drip a little wax from each of the candles in. Extinguish the candles and incense and fill the watering can up to full. Pour out the water over your new plants repeating the above charm three times and bury the crystal either in a plant bed or a pot.

Digging in the earth, getting dirt beneath your nails, watching something green take root and grow because of you, transforming your surroundings with living things can all be spiritual experiences. You are close to the element of Earth, you are sowing and growing your magick. I was always taught that The Goddess loves plants, trees and flowers. This is a way to feel close to Her and close to nature, as well as the God, who is of course, sometimes known as Jack O the Green. As you are working in your garden you may think of the toil as being dedicated to Them, and it is possible to slip into a meditative or trance like state as you garden. A sunny green patch is a wonderful thing mentally and the physical exercise is good for you too. Additionally, if you can spend some time in a wooded or forested area this can be an almost healing experience, the quiet, the pure oxygen produced by the trees and plants, the fact that some of them are very old... Highly recommended!

NOTE: The use of marijuana, magic mushrooms and morning glory seeds for magick and/or visions is neither condemned nor condoned. Some modern sects of witchcraft seriously frown upon the use of mind altering substances of any kind, but when you get right down to it the caffeine in tea, coffee, and many pops is a mind altering substance. I will say that doing anything illegal is never a great idea and that mushrooms are very dangerous. They are, in fact, poison, and can cause long lasting mental effects that can be devastating. Morning glory seeds are now almost always treated with a substance that stops them from rotting but also makes a person very ill. Marijuana, while sometimes good for meditating and vision work is illegal in most countries.

7: A WITCH'S COLOUR WHEEL

There is much talk about and use of correspondences in magick and witchcraft. Plants, stones, animals, pictures, shells, metals, incenses, woods and many other things can be incorporated into spells to strengthen and focus them, One of the most powerful of the correspondences is colour. Throughout human history colour has been used in rituals, festivals, religion and magick. Colour's use in healing can be traced to Ancient Egypt and modern studies have found that various colours can have soothing, calming, or stimulating effects. Witches have always known that each colour of the spectrum vibrates with a different energy. These energies can be utilized in spell work and everyday living. It can be as simple as a choice of what shade of T-shirt to put on in the morning or as complex as the different colours used in making your marriage candle.

The trio of white, red and black represents the triple aspect of the Goddess (Maiden, Mother, Crone). Similarly, the trio of green, blue and purple signify the triple God. Black and White provide a balance and represent the God and Goddess. Basically, the different wavelengths that colours vibrate on indeed give off different energies. This is one of the most accessible forms of magick, one that can be practiced every day by everyone. There are thousands of books and websites that state what each colour "means" and of course, some of that information is good and valid, some is hogwash. As with everything in the Craft it is important to note how these feel to you. You will know what is right.

Blue

Azure, Azul, Turquoise, Royal, Navy, Baby, Sky, Aqua, Periwinkle, Sapphire,

My personal favourite of all the colours!

Resonates with: Calm, health, healing, wisdom, water, love.

Associated with: the West quarter, The Water Element, water signs (Pisces, Cancer, Scorpio) Undines (water Elementals), Fall, the Squire aspect of the Triple God.

Very often the best colour for healing, blue is good for inflammation, childbirth, cuts and scrapes, fevers, stings and bites and any affliction that is "hot" arthritis, strains, etc.

Wearing blue is good to show others that you speak the truth and can be trusted. This is no doubt why it is said to be good to wear blue to court.

Good for tranquillity, patience and safety.

In aura's it's said to mean good health, intelligence, love, peace and wisdom, although dark blue-black can indicate disbelief, nervousness, or a person feeling unsure.

Good for protecting your reputation, for poetry, truth, wisdom, loyalty, fidelity. For meditation and learning. To defeat an enemy. To protect hearth and home as well as loved ones. Justice. Long associated with boys and can represent them in spell work (as well as a man, father, or the God) but it is also a Goddess colour. Blue is a wonderful colour for promoting peace. Great to wear for a job interview, to work, or on a date. Great for improving psychic powers, Divining, studying, memory and rest as well as love. A perfect colour for sheets, pillow cases and bedroom walls, especially if you are having trouble sleeping. Use blue ink for studying, school work, writing down dreams, and court papers. (Unless you are required to use black!)

The numbers 7 and 11. Litha.

Red

Crimson, Scarlet, Blood, Fiery, Barn, Alizarin, Ruby, Wine, Cardinal, Maroon.

Resonates with: Passion, love, lust. fire, anger, intensity, warriors.

Associated with: The South quarter, Fire, fire signs (Aries, Leo, and Sagittarius) Salamanders (Fire Elementals), Summer, the Mother aspect of the Goddess.

Red is a great colour for love magick, for passionate sexual love between two people. Great for strength and vigour. For courage. For ailments of the blood or ailments that weaken or are "cold"

Use red to promote action. Leadership and the Planet Mars. Dark reds and maroons are associated with Scorpios. For life-renewal, and expanding. Signifies the Mother aspect of the triple Goddess. Maturity, confidence and knowing oneself. Sex magick. Red can represent a woman or mother in a spell.

In auras it is said to mean vitality, love, passion, leadership, confidence and may indicate rage.

Wear red to take charge and lead a group or to display confidence. A great colour for sports teams or if you are playing sports casually with friends. Wear red to get noticed!

Attraction and the masculine power. Love and lust. A red candle is almost a requirement of a love spell. Luck. Summer. Deep and lasting affection. Power and victory. Also associated with anger and hatred, whatever emotions are evoked with red energy they are sure to be powerful, passionate ones! Use red ink for love spells, sex spells, and anything to do with sports teams.

The numbers 3 and 27.

Samhain, Lammas, Mabon.

Green

Sea foam, Jade, Emerald, Hunter, Grass, Swamp, Kelly, Forest, Military, Frogs, Lizards.

Resonates with: Nature, Earth, environment, health, luck, prosperity, abundance.

Associated with: the North Quarter, Earth, earth signs (Taurus, Virgo, Capricorn), Gnomes (Earth Elementals), Spring, and also winter in the Circle, the Son aspect of the Triple God, the natural world.

Green is another good colour for healing. Also especially good for wealth, prosperity, good fortune, luck. Anything to do with the world around you. Good for headaches. Who hasn't heard of "going green"? Our planet, the environment, doing good for the world, giving back, protecting the ecology. The Green Man or Jack O' the Green or the God. Spring, the planets Venus and Mercury. Agricultural magick. Any spell work for prosperity to bring money (with gold or silver), to find a job or a new source of income. Sometimes when I'm short of money and am not quite sure how I am going to pay for everything I make my shopping lists in green ink and somehow, I usually find I am able to purchase everything on the list before long. Also it is good to write your rough drafts in green ink, anything you might want a little extra luck with such as business proposals or important school papers.

In aura's it can indicate harmony, comfort, assurance and peace, although it can also mean jealousy. Who hasn't also heard of green with envy?

Herb and plant magick. The outdoors. Connecting with nature and Wheel of the Year. Fertility and finance. A green candle is almost a necessity in prosperity and fertility magick. Works great with blue and white in healing rituals.

Wear green to be calm, assured, and attract good luck and good fortune, as well as when asking for a loan or a raise.

The numbers 8 and 14. Dwarves and other Little People. A

God and a Goddess colour. Yule and Ostara.

Great for weather magick!

Yellow

Topaz, Sun, Sunny, Buttercup. Daffodil. Dandelion, Sulphur, Butter.

Resonates with: Confidence, beauty, goodness, friendliness, light and life. My least favourite colour, I also associate it with sickness, jaundice and jealousy.

Associated with: The Eastern Quarter, Air, Air Signs (Gemini, Libra, Aquarius). Spring, innocence. Persuasion, charm, attraction. Intellect. The energy of the Sun and the God. Self-esteem, beauty. Good for divination.

A yellow aura is said to be a very good one, denoting joy, happiness, a "sunny nature," and kindness, but as I said, there is something I very much dislike about the colour, and a yellow aura can also indicate feeling unsure or illness.

Said to be good (with blue) for stress and learning.

Wear yellow if you are lacking in self-esteem and want to be charming and confident. Good for beauty magick, as well as persuasion and self-confidence spells. Yellow is meant to be a cheering, happy colour that helps with depression. It's good to paint the inside of your house yellow when you live in a grey or cold climate, especially the kitchen. All magick related to the home. Use yellow ink for home projects and lists of home or decorating supplies, as well as beauty and charm spells.

The number 6.

Beltane.

White

Alabaster, porcelain, snow, milk, quartz, snow drops, lilies, the moon, diamonds, pearls, ivory, wine.

Resonates with: Peace and harmony, calm, purity, spirituality, cleanliness and clarity, protection.

Associated with: The Goddess, especially the Maiden aspect. Winter, prayer, purity, the After-Life, cold.

Good for all magick. You can't go wrong by adding a white candle, cloth, or ribbons to your spell work. The yin side of the balance. Freedom, illumination, peace and Power. The Great Mysteries. Intuition, Love. Can be used to symbolize a person, place or thing. Use a white candle if you can't get the other colour or aren't sure what colour to use. Can be charged with the Power of any of the other colour energies. A white candle is sometimes used to symbolize the Goddess, truth, purity and sincerity.

A white aura is said to denote knowledge, spirituality, peacefulness, calm, or a "good continence." Favourable.

Perfect for Moon magick, Full Moon rituals, meditation. Great for cleansing and purifying. To attune with the Goddess.

Wear white to show your innocence, purity and truthfulness, or to make you seem larger. Obviously, you can't use white ink on white paper, but you could try sometime to get some dark paper and a white pen at an art supply shop for spell work relating to the Goddess and purity.

Protection. The number 1.

Imbolc, Beltane and Litha.

Black

Night, Midnight, Onyx, Obsidian, Dark, Deep, Ebony, Noir.

Resonates with: Calm, Power, possibilities, mystery, protection, magick, beginnings.

Associated with: The God, Scorpios, The Yang aspect of the Balance, The Crone aspect of the Triple Goddess. Masculine and feminine, everything, the oneness of all.

Very unfortunately the colour black has some negative connotations. But it is a protective colour. Black can be used as a banishing colour; it is used to return negativity to the sender.

The God is sometimes represented on the altar by a black candle, but black also represents the Dark Goddess as well as the Crone aspect. Also associated with winter like white.

Infinity, rebirth, wisdom. Time, the first stage of the working. Destiny. destroying bad habits. Fight negativity and protect. Power. Good for wounded pride. Use for magickal protection. The void, space, eternity. Lack of falsehood. Rest. Investigation. To calm down. A black aura is rarely seen but may indicate spirituality or neutrality.

Wear black to protect yourself from negativity, to rest and recharge, to be strong and spiritual. A very powerful colour. The After-Life, the dead. The dark. Endless possibilities. Use black ink for banishing negativity, business dealings, moon or sleep magick, and, of course on documents where it is required!

The numbers, 4 and 9,

Samhain.

Avoid over-use. Use with white to make sure there is balance.

Pink

Rose, Shell, Magenta, Shocking, Pearl, Tourmaline.

Resonates with: Peaceful love, friendship, devotion, adoration, affection.

Associated with: the gentle, the benign, love, friendship, motherhood.

Ah pink. While it is true every love spell certainly contains a red candle and red correspondences, no spell for true love would be complete without pink (unless you are doing a spell for a one-night stand!) Passion and lust (red) are absolutely fantastic and important components in a relationship, but so too must there be friendly and affectionate love (pink). This is tenderness, devotion and friendship. In fact, for spell work involving making new platonic friends and attracting all people to you pink is your colour. A pink aura is said to denote love as well as success, cheerfulness, joy, and friendliness.

Honour. Famial love and long lasting love. Friendship, harmony. Girls, woman and the Goddess. Loved ones. Humility and morality. Rosiness. Think of the term "looking at life through rose coloured glasses" who doesn't want to feel that way sometimes? A very benign and beneficial colour.

Wear pink to attract friendliness, benevolence, love and to show your honour. Use pink ink for the sweet and tender parts of love spells, as well as friendship and attraction spells, and for things related to girls and birthdays.

The number 5.

Litha.

Purple

Violet, Indigo, Lilac, Lavender, Puce, Aubergine, Eggplant, Purple Martins.

Resonates with: Spirituality, knowledge, wisdom. intelligence, forgiveness, fairness, rightness.

Associated with: Royalty, humility, the Ancients, Wisdom, Power, the planet Jupiter, The Great Mysteries. The Spirit or fifth Element, the Sage aspect of the triple God.

A great colour for business dealings and wisdom. Learning, higher learning. Calling to the Ancients, ancestors, the God and Goddess. Peace, serenity, healing. Invoking or calling to the Spirit. Charitable work, other good works, dream magick. Devotion, especially religious. Only royalty were allowed to wear purple in the English court in the sixteenth century. Justice and anything to do with the Government.

Wear purple in business and government dealings to give you an advantage as well as for spiritual workings and dream magick.

A purple aura is said to denote spirituality, wisdom, calmness, fairness, as well as maturity and good humour.

Purple is the colour of ambition and progress but also of

spirituality and peace. Justice and very importantly forgiveness. Use purple in a spell if you want someone to forgive you or if need to forgive someone. Use purple ink in these spells, as well as for Spirituality magick, to attain higher knowledge, and in Government dealings (unless you are required to use black ink that is!).

The number 7 (blue-purple).

Orange

Tangerine, carrot, amber, citrine, flame, pumpkin, marmalade, tiger.

Resonates with: heat, warmth, the ability to overcome, confidence.

Associated with: fire and happiness. Luxury. The Sun, beating the odds.

For protection, facing challenges. The 'Easy Life.' To help seal spell. To represent the God in his fiery solar aspect. Luck, Prosperity.

Adaptability, attraction, confidence. Encouragement and stimulation. Spirituality. Opportunities. Breaks blockages. Material gain. An orange aura denotes harmony and vitality but also pride and anger and sometimes a lack of intellect or clear thinking.

Wear orange for confidence, to "face up" to someone or something, for courage, and for anything connected to material gain.

To remove feelings of abandonment. Use orange ink for spells relating to better living, to overcome a challenge or to get over someone or something, writings related to luxury, as well as for lists of luxury items you may want to acquire.

The number 12.

Mabon, Lammas and Samhain.

Gray

Charcoal, Pewter, Ash, Iron, Slate, Granite, Wolf, Sharks.

Resonates with: Stability, slowing down a situation or person, invisibility.

Associated with: Invisibility. reflection, brilliance, correcting instability, weather magick. There is not a great deal associated with the colour gray in my family tradition, but I felt it was important to include it if only because of its power of invisibility. Wear gray when you want to blend in, pass under the radar, go unnoticed. Honestly, this really works well. With a little glamory and gray clothes you can be nearly invisible and forgettable. Interestingly, the colour gray is associated with glamory. A gray aura may indicate calm, assurance, or someone in the twilight of this incarnation. Gray is also used in Weather magick, calming a situation down, and preventing things from moving too fast. Use gray ink for weather magick and spells to slow something down.

Brown

Dun, Tan, Beige, Earth, Bronze, Bear.

Resonates with: Security, support, nature.

Associated with: The sign of Capricorn, the Earth, animals, gardens, weather, plants, gnomes.

Uncertainty. Soothes emotional upsets. Nature magick. The God. Working with the Earth, the forest.

Great for working with animals and in animal and Totem magick. Weather magick.

Elementals of Earth such as Gnomes and Fairies. Magick for, and relating to the home. A brown aura can indicate steadiness, dedication and devotion, but may also indicate tiredness or illness.

Wear brown, perhaps to a job interview or in business dealings to show your responsibility and practicality. Use brown ink for a resume rough draft and for home renovation plans. Mabon.

Silver

Steel, Sparkle, Stars, Tin, Shimmer, Ghostly, Lightning.

Resonates with: The Moon, The Goddess, prosperity, freedom, spirituality.

Associated with: The night, astral travel, The Goddess, Moon magick, Reflection.

A Goddess colour. Purity, abundance. Used with green and gold in money and prosperity magick. Used with white in moon magick and Full Moon Rituals. Star magick. Reality and reflection. Restore balance and destroy delusions. Endurance. Peace. Personal growth and learning. Meditation and connection to the Spirit. Cancellation. A silver aura denotes idealism, energy, spiritualism, quick wits. Divine Mysteries and higher learning. Wear some silver for spirituality, to be noticed, to be calm and lucky. Use silver ink for Goddess spells and to connect with the Goddess, as well as for luck and to bring riches.

The number 2.

Lucky keys and coins. Yule.

Gold

Brass, Shine, Flash, Brilliance, Gild, or Gilt.

Resonates with: Power, the God, the Sun, prosperity, riches.

Associated with: the sun, the God, the day, Power, money, luck,

Used with green and silver in prosperity magick. Used to charm and persuade. Used to protect. Earthly wealth. Good luck or good fortune. Wear gold to realize your full potential, to attract wealth, and for luck. Lucky tokens or coins.

A gold aura indicates talent, an open mind, and mental richness.

Truth and Attraction. Use gold ink for prosperity magick and luck.

The number 6.

8: A WITCH'S STONES AND CRYSTALS

Stones are a witch's natural ally. Easy to collect, abundant, and full of a virtual feast of untapped energy, they are everywhere, literally underfoot. All one has to be to make use of them is slightly sensitive. Next time you are at a seashore, by a lake, stream or river, in a wood or a park, or even in a gravel driveway collect a handful of stones. Clean them in running water (under a tap will do) and roll them through your hands. Close your eyes and hold each one in turn. Make note of their shape and colour. What attracted you to them in the first place? What do you feel when you hold each one? Are they emanating a particular energy?

You may not be adept at discovering this right away. It can take some time to develop this skill. If you feel an attachment or a strong energy from any that you have collected, cleanse and consecrate it (them) and keep for your personal use. Small stones can be cleansed by passing them through a white candle's flame, the smoke of a purifying incense such as sage, and being sprinkled with sea salt and chalice water. You can also leave them in a bowl of salt in the light of a waning moon for seven nights. Then do a simple dedication, asking the Lady and Lord to bless them for your personal, magickal and beneficial use. It is said in my family that a stone should be charged or activated before use. This can be done in a Circle or at your altar. Be sure to charge the stone according to your magickal intent, such as for protection, love, healing, whatever you are going to use it for. Pouring energy from the middle of your forehead (your "Third eye") and your hands as you concentrate on surrounding the stone with light in the correct colour (blue or white for healing, red or pink for love etc.), feel the power awaken in the stone. You may wish to carry the stone with you for a few days so it will continue to absorb energies from you. For even as stones are able to magickally project energy they are also receptive (some more than others, like anything) and can be filled with the power of your intent.

Some of the very best magick stones are found in this way because you have selected them personally. They are then placed on the altar during spell craft, or Circles, used on the table during Sabbats (maybe a stone you found in the summer would be appropriate at Yule, to remind you of summer's return, or a pebble found at a cemetery might be used at Samhain and so on), added to pouches, brought to healings, used for divination, placed under a pillow for dream magick, or simply carried in a pocket or purse as a talisman or luck piece. Very versatile indeed! Plus, they need not cost anything.

Stone magick is one of the oldest forms of magick. Stones have been used as amulets and talisman back to time immemorial. A lot has been said in the last few decades about the use of crystal in healing as a sort of flaky, silly, stereotype. I suppose crystal healing may have been embraced by a few light weight types but that is neither here nor there considering it can work.

Of course, different stones are used for different things as they naturally possess different energies. This may have something to do with the way a stone is formed. For example, hardened lava is said to have projective protective powers, i.e. the power to violently repel negativity.

In the section on correspondences (*A Witch's Spell Correspondences*) I will be including more stone types according to what their properties are best suited to, but I'd like to go into a few of the main ones I like to work with here. Some gems are relatively inexpensive and are versatile enough to be worth adding to your collection. Quartz crystals contain some of most powerful, tap-able energies and are useful to any witch. They are almost a must for healing spells and rituals and are sacred to the Goddess. Bring a healing-charged quartz with you to a sick person's bedside. If they are open-minded place it on their forehead while you concentrate on them being well and whole. See if you can get them to keep it with them, under a pillow or by the bed. Crystal quartz can be used as a stand-in for any other stone (can be charged with *any* magickal intent) can be used for altering consciousness, spirituality, meditation, to increase the power of spells, to honour or communicate with the dead, for scrying (as in the infamous crystal ball). The list goes on and on. A quartz (or a smoky or milky or rose quartz) crystal's power is enhanced by leaving it in the light of a waxing or full moon. In fact, I like to "bathe" my crystals regularly by leaving them in the moonlight to recharge and clean them. Some will say that quartz needs to be left in a cloth bag when not in use but I have never found this to be true as long as they are left in the moonlight every few months to refresh them. Boil water and steep a (clean) quartz crystal in it. Allow it to cool and remove the stone. Drink as a restorative tonic. Whether polished or natural quartz crystals are relatively inexpensive and a great asset in magickal workings. Of course, if you find them yourself they can be even more potent.

Rose quartz is another good one to have around. It is hugely beneficial to all kinds of love magick, whether friendly or passionate. It promotes good will, happiness, joy, and faith. It is great for fidelity magick and is just a generally feel good stone.

Amethyst is fairly easy to obtain and can be used against all types of pain, physical, spiritual, mental, for dream magick, against alcoholism and drunkenness, for courage, protection and happiness. It helps to prevent stress and enhances your spiritual side.

Lapis Lazuli is expensive but can be a good one to try to get, it is very useful in healing, especially soothing, calming types of healing and against fevers, stings and burns. It is good for building your psychic powers, for protection, and joy, and aids in divination when placed nearby.

Some "stones" are not stones at all. Amber, coral, pearls, mica, fossils and other non-stones all have their place in magickal workings, as listed in the correspondence chapter. Amber, for instance, is a great aid to beauty magick, and is also useful for love and attaining and keeping great health. Be sure not to get plastic when buying amber. A note about coral: Please only collect coral which washes up on beaches. The world's coral reefs are being severely depleted due to pollution and climate changes, and the last thing a witch should do is add to this problem. If you are buying coral and are in doubt of whether it was harvested from a living reef please leave it behind. That being said, coral that has washed up on shore is good to use for learning, to honour the dead and for calmness.

I grew up with a lot of granite or "bedrock" from the Pre-Cambrian shield. It is great for protection, to aid in sleeping, to hold and rub as a worry stone, and can be charged with almost any magickal intent much like crystal quartz. River stones or pebbles from the sea that have been naturally smoothed in the water make fantastic worry stones. These can be carried in a pocket, concealed if you choose, and rubbed when you are nervous. Of course you don't want to keep your hands stuffed in your pockets during a job interview or date, but they are wonderful for waiting rooms, or before you meet someone.

Turquoise is great for protection, love, healing, and is said to protect a horse back rider from falls. Place it on a sick person's forehead or carry it to them when you go to heal. Jade is wonderful for wisdom, money magick, love and success. Agates are generally lucky, especially moss or lace agates. There is a "new" gem stone called ammolite that is actually a fossil. So far it has been found in only one place, which is a lake in Alberta, Canada. It comes from a fairly common shelled sea creature that lived 100 million years ago. For some reason in this particular part of the world these creature's shells, when they became fossilized, turned into a rainbow of colours. Ammolite can be red, orange, green, purple, blue, gold or all of these in one piece and is very good for improving your will power and ordering your life. When given as a gift it means eternal love. Onyx is generally lucky and makes a fine spell booster. Obsidian (sacred to some North America First Nations tribes) aids in divination and scrying and is protective.

Jet is said to be the "Witch's stone" and be especially lucky for witches to possess. I do not tend to agree, but it is worth noting I have a bad association and may be biased. Similarly, opals were and are considered terrible luck in my family tradition, and as result I know little of them, except that I won't own or wear one, but that may not be true for everyone. Moonstones are thought to be ill-omened by some, but others state that they are good for garden magick, sleep, love, weight loss and maintaining a youthful aspect.

In terms of precious stones you may own, buy, or receive in jewellery, diamonds are especially good for fidelity (no doubt why they are so popular in engagement rings, although one wonders why it's mostly women who wear them!) They are also good for love magick, for deeper bonding, strength, sexual problems and issues, getting back together and peace. Emeralds are very lucky and signify lasting love, are useful for money magick, luck, business, as well as helping your memory and developing your psychic power. Sapphires are also good for fidelity and strengthening a love or pair-bond, for healing, and meditation. Star sapphires are said to attract new love to you. All sapphires promote social discourse and a healthy social life. Good in legal matters and to attract wealth, sapphires are even said to warn you of a lover's infidelity by changing their hue. Rubies were said long ago to be for and signify the virtuous woman, and are good for protection, passion, and to guard you against bad luck. They protect the wearer and are even said to protect your house. Garnets are good for blood diseases, astral travel or "flying," bravery, and lust. Tanzanite, which is a stunning purple-blue colour, is great for love, friendship, good health and longevity.

My personal favourite gem (well, one of them, I confess a deep love of most gem stones) is blue topaz, good for calming, alleviating stress, weight loss, depression, and to aid the digestive system.

There are many fine resources available to tell you what each stone and crystal is "for." For my purpose I will say that rocks, crystals, minerals, and stones, because they are of the Earth and are created by nature are finely attuned to it. They are in harmony with older, deeper, rhythms and they hold untold power that can be utilized by a clever, dedicated witch. Carry a small stone in your pocket or purse. Slip one under your pillow. Build your collection of gathered and/or bought stones. Familiarize yourself with their feelings and energies. Know what each type or individual stone means to you. Then draw one or three from a bag in a very simple divination. Use a black or dark stone for 'no' and a light or white for 'yes' (or vice versa). Some use a white stone to represent the Goddess and a black stone the God. Despite all the good and valuable knowledge about kinds of stones and their uses only you will instinctively feel where each stone's power lies.

Colour magick can be utilized with stones, of course. Note that rose quartz; a lovely rose-colored stone is beneficial in much of the same types of magick as the colour pink. Similarly, many blue stones are good for healing, peace and love, and green stones for luck and money. Crystal quartz, like the colour white, can be charged with and boost any kind of magick, and so on. If in doubt about a stone's best use, check the corresponding colour's use.

How nice it can be to live in a stone house! Try to arrange to spend even one night in a stone house and see if it doesn't provoke any special feelings or perhaps dreams.

There is much said and written about birthstones. The general idea is that they are especially beneficial when worn or carried by the person of the sun sign that they govern. I have found, however, that there are a lot of discrepancies in this field. For example, as a Pisces I have been told at various times that my birthstone is an Amethyst, an Aquamarine, a Bloodstone, and a Lapis. I believe some of confusion stems from the fact that there are ancient and modern versions of birthstones, and that sometimes they are determined by month, and sometimes by zodiac sign, such as Amethyst for February and Amethyst for Pisces. Below is a list for the most common birthstone listings by month, but as to which, if any, is 100 percent correct, your feelings are as good as mine. I find that aquamarine resonates nicely with me and have noticed that lots of people born in the month of March, both Pisces and Aries, seem to love the blue-green colour scheme. In terms of choosing which will be yours it must be a personal decision. You might choose to carry or wear or own one, all, or none of the choices. Try to handle at least one example of each stone and see if it "speaks" to you or awakens anything in you. See which, if any, create a feeling or response. This will be the best way to determine your lucky birthstone.

January: Chalcedony, Garnet, Rose Quartz, Emerald.

February: Amethyst, Onyx, Bloodstone, Clear Quartz.

March: Aquamarine, Bloodstone, Jasper, Lapis, Jade, Amethyst.

April: Diamond, Smoky Quartz, Sapphire, Opal, Sardonyx.

May: Topaz, Emerald, Agate, Sapphire, Chyrsoprase.

June: Opal, Pearl, Alexandrite, Morganite, Moonstone, Agate, Turquoise.

July: Chalcedony, Ruby, Carnelian, Onyx, Emerald.

August: Peridot, Sardonyx, Diamond, Topaz, Jasper.

September: Sapphire, Lapis, Carnelian, Emerald.

October: Unakite, Tourmaline, Beryl, Bloodstone, Jasper, Amethyst.

November: Topaz, Citrine, Pearl, Sapphire.

December: Tanzanite, Zircon, Turquoise, Ruby, Sapphire.

9: A WITCH'S SPELL CORRESPONDENCES

Much is accomplished in witchcraft and magick through the aid of correspondences. Correspondences can be objects that remind you of or evoke a person, place, or thing, colours, rocks, crystals, numbers, plants, photos, pictures, symbols, pictographs, elements, deity related and many more. The idea behind their use is that they resonate with, project, or attract different energies. These energies then draw in like energy (like attracts like, this is an important principle in my family's tradition) or repel other types of energy. They are used in spells, on the altar, in the Circle, in charm bags, poppets, jars, during rituals and ceremonies. Many of these spell boosters come down from "the old aunts" as well as my mother and grandfather, but it is worth noting that these chapters in my own Book of Shadows are always being added to. Through trial and error, observation and continuing reading and learning I am always discovering new possibilities and you will too. We have looked briefly at stones, plants and colours. Now, in reverse, we look at examples of the most powerful of my family's traditional uses of correspondences for Love, Healing and Health, Protection, Spirituality, Prosperity, Weather, Luck, Beauty or Looking Good, and Travel.

Love

We'll start with perhaps the most popular and sought after type of magick and charm. Spells for love can be very effective if we bear in mind that it is rather unethical to target one's power on a specific person unless we are already in a relationship with them. Consider how you would feel if someone took away your will and choice and you found yourself crazy for someone you would not normally consider. So unless you are involved with or married to someone and strengthening an existing love bond, it is better to focus your energy on attracting the right sort of person into your life.

Use the colour red for passion, love, lust, and strong, lasting love. Use the colour pink for friendly love, trust, and affection. The colour blue works for harmonious love, and the colours white or silver for asking the Goddess to bless your love, as well as white for love of another on a spiritual level. Pink or red can be used to represent a woman and blue a man, green for a young man. Use black or gold for the God's help in love matters. The Goddesses Aphrodite, Isis, Venus, Bridgit (or Bride, Brid, or Brigit, always pronounced Breed in my family), Hathor, Bronwen, Maeve, Freyja and others are helpful in love magick. The Egyptian Goddess Selket is said to be the protector of marriage and sexual love. Doves, sparrows, dogs or wolves (especially in matters concerning fidelity, loyalty, and blended families; i.e. helping a new man or woman to love your children). For long lasting love use any animals that mate for life such as swans, eagles, and again wolves.

Agates, jasper (especially red jasper) and rose quartz. Rose quartz is very powerful in love spells and charms. Keeping one under your pillow while you visualize the type of love partner you would like can help you draw love. As well, empowering two rose quartz' for harmonious and joyous love and giving one to your partner and keeping one for yourself is a powerful charm. Rose quartz is great in love pouches and bundles. Also topaz, (any colour), turquoise, rubies and heart shaped stones of all kinds, either naturally formed of manmade. Jade, diamonds for love and fidelity, sapphires for spells to strengthen couples. Use star sapphires to attract love. Rubies, alexandrite. Carnelian can help return passion to a relationship. Lapis lazuli is useful both in spells to attract new love and to promote fidelity and harmony in established couples. Malachite worn against your skin increases your capacity to receive love and draw love to you. Pearls are reputed to be useful in love magick, but I tend to worry that as their creator must be killed to collect them this could cause negative effects. Always cleanse them before use with special attention to the creature that made them in your thanks. Pink tourmalines and onyx. Any pink or red stones and some white or blue ones, any stone that gives you a feeling of love or a warm affection. As always, charge the stones with your magickal intent before use.

Pictures and photographs, either of your partner, the two of you together, or the type of partner you want. Pictographs of their astrological sign symbol perhaps twined with your own. Your initials twined together as well. Pictures or figurines of wolves, dogs, swans, sparrows, or your own spirit animal along with the animal spirit of your partner or the type of spirit animal of the partner you would wish to have. Knots, especially those known as 'love knots' using red or pink cords or ribbons, and sometimes knotting together two items representing each partner. Small items from your life together, or that come from or represent your partner. Obviously heart symbols, pictures, representations and pictographs, containing your initials, or two hearts twined together and slightly overlapped, sometimes with a line running outside the two and binding them like a hug. Invoking pentagrams for success in your love ventures. Spiral designs, two circles joined and overlapping, and male and female signs drawn together overlapping (or two male symbols or two female symbols as the case may be). Use red ink, pink ink, dove's blood ink, or white ink on red or pink paper.

Strawberries, apples and tomatoes, which were once known as 'love apples'. An old charm states that if a young woman would know the initial of her future mate (it can be a first or last name and is fairly open to interpretation) she should peel an apple in one long, continuous strand and toss the peel over her right shoulder. The peel will form the letter on ground behind her. This is best done on New Year's Eve or at Imbolc. Jasmine, red or pink roses, hibiscus, lavender, and orris (iris) root, powdered, are especially potent for all sorts of love magick. Daisies, mistletoe, poppies, rosemary, lilies, trilliums, tulips, vervain, cloves, cinnamon, passionflower, daffodils and passion fruit. Peaches, peach blossoms and peach wood, as well as magnolia flowers and roots. Kava kava, a plant found in the south pacific and brewed in a tea makes a fine aphrodisiac, as my husband and I discovered when offered some at a ceremony in Fiji. A woman can wash her hair in a thyme infusion to make her more attractive to the opposite sex, or either gender can use thyme in cooking for love meals. Laurel leaves burned in an open fire are said to attract a lover, as are pink or rubrem lilies worn in the hair. Garlic is useful in love spells and love cooking. Gardenia flowers are very potent, as well as sandalwood, basil, lemon balm, and ginger, often cut into 9 or 27 pieces. Ylang ylang is good for partnership spells, and crocus helps to attract new love. Asparagus stirs up bodily lust when eaten, and violets can be used in a spell for the same purpose. Honey, used both in love spells and meals for lovers, or a pinch of brown sugar to "keep things sweet" between you can be added to pouches and the like.

The numbers 3, 9, and 27. It is said to be especially favourable to work love magick on a Friday. Also, it is good to work it when the moon is in Libra or Taurus, or for new love with the moon in Aquarius. As usual, the new and waxing moon are for creating, growing and expanding, while the waning moon is less favourable for love spells, as it is for decreasing and banishing. The exception might be to use a waning moon to diminish something in a partnership, such as discord or time apart. Prepared love or aphrodisia oils, powders, herb blends, and candles are widely available over the Internet. Make sure you cleanse them and infuse them with your own special energy before use, perhaps adding your own dried herbs or petals to blends, powders or oils. Lavender, jasmine, gardenia, or prepared love oils can be great for anointing oneself or any candles and crystals you may be using, add a piece of orris root to the oil if you can, and use lemon oil for attraction. Use oil of linden flower containing a piece of magnolia root in spells to keep a lover faithful. Prepared love drawing powders, often containing powdered sandalwood, frankincense and rose oil can be sprinkled around the altar and added to pouches along with orris root.

An enterprising witch could devise an excellent spell for strengthening their relationship with these correspondences. Pictures of a couple together, pictures of each, bound facing one another with pink and blue ribbons, rose quartz, orris root and jasmine flowers, astrological and heart pictographs, perhaps those of intertwined hearts, a pubic hair from each partner knotted together, bodily items such as hair clippings, nail cuttings or old teeth, red and pink wax, and small items from their life together (a match book from the place they met, a small candy of a favourite type to keep things sweet, possibly from a box one gave the other, a stone or some sand from a trip together, even a tissue used to clean up after sex) can be cleansed, empowered, and sewn up into a red cloth pouch with red or pink thread as a very powerful togetherness spell. Even preparing for the ritual is part of the magick. Buying the cloth, assembling the items, planning the timing (say on a Friday, with a waxing moon in Libra?) can prepare you to create a powerful spell. Each item can be passed through the smoke of lavender, strawberry or jasmine incense, over the flame of red and pink candles, dipped into a chalice of spring water (or sprinkled with droplets of the water) and sprinkled with sea salt. It would be fantastic to do this together; if possible, even sewing alternate stitches when closing the fourth side of the pouch or bundle.

Another wonderful thing to do with love correspondences is to make a lovers dinner to be enjoyed together, perhaps including oysters and asparagus for lust, as well as rosemary, thyme, and apples in the main dish, and perhaps chocolate dipped strawberries for dessert. As you prepare this repast for (or with) your lover focus on increasing the love, lust, and good feelings in your relationship, infusing the food with your magickal intent.

For someone looking for new love, an altar spell with pink and red candles, perhaps with laurel leaves, a piece of malachite or star sapphire, frankincense, strawberry or lavender incense, lemon oil, crocus flowers, and pictures, maybe from magazines, of the type of lover you seek can be excellent and effective. Be careful, when using magazine pictures, not to focus too hard on the actual person in the image, but rather the qualities they have that you desire. Concentrate on the love you have to give. Gaze into a mirror and think of how you wish to appear to potential partners. Visualize yourself happily partnered with the kind of man or woman you would be fulfilled with. Maybe respectfully ask the Lady and Lord to help to bring them into your life. Carry a small item from you ritual in a pocket or purse to help you focus on drawing that person to you as you seek them with an open heart and mind, and above all, remember they are out there.

Protection

Protection implies care of a spiritual, mental, or physical nature. Obviously if someone is in immediate physical danger the best course of action is to involve police, fire, or medical authorities. But perhaps you're walking alone in a dark street, or waiting for help to arrive. Perhaps you think a co-worker is jealous and trying to get you fired, or your child is being bullied at school. In these instances and countless others protection magick can come into play.

The main type of protection magick I was taught to use is a white or blue "shield" usually built around a person or place. This involves closing your eyes and visualizing a thick aura of blue or white light, strong, sparkling, powerful, and completely enclosing said person or place. You may want to open and close your eyes several times, and squint a few times to help you get it in place. If it is a person you are shielding you imagine every part of their body in turn surrounded by this coloured light, and if it is a place you may wish to walk around the building creating your shield. Pour your mental energy toward the person or place (or even an object), actually seeing this light and knowing it will protect them and keep them safe and untouched. A black shield may also be used to repel negativity when you are aware that there is intent to harm taking place. You can shield yourself in such a way as well. White light is best for general protection of all kinds, while blue is more for physical protection and keep someone in good health or to keep a place safe from physical harm such as storm damage. This technique may take some practise but can be very effective if you keep at it.

The colour white then, is great for protection, and the colour black to repel or return to sender, and the colour blue against physical harm. Gray can help you be invisible from those that would do you harm. The Goddesses Diana or Artemis, Hathor, Athene, Demeter (for protection of women), Nekhebet and the Valkyries to lend you fearlessness.

Agates, moonstones (although, conversely thought to bring ill-luck. Handle a piece and see how it feels to you), cat's eye, garnets, especially when worn, and especially during the dark street walk and as protection when worn and against insect stings and bites. Stones with natural holes in them, tiger's eye, onyx, rubies, amber necklaces, especially worn by children. Crystal quartz can be charged to protect a wearer or a home, or a personal item such as a purse, back pack or lap top case. Flint used in amulets of protection or placed above a doorway. Pieces of iron or iron nails. Citrine is said to protect against nightmares when worn or placed under a pillow (although I still have the odd one). A piece of lava is great for all kinds of protection, while jasper can return negativity to its sender. Mother of pearl (carefully cleansed) protects babies and young children, jade worn or carried guards against accidents of all types. Mica, and obsidian, especially carved into the shape of an arrow head. Turquoise can be used to protect against violence and accidents, especially while riding horses. Any black or white stones. Salt is great too, especially sprinkled about the home or property.

Frankincense incense, as well as patchouli. Sage incense, bundles or leaves are fantastic to cleanse, purify, drive away negativity and protect. Grow sage in your house or garden for this purpose. Rosemary, rue, wisteria, clover, lily of the valley, periwinkles, and lilac. Geraniums planted on the property protect it and its inhabitants. Ash wood (although not broken from a living tree), Myrrh incense. Lavender is great for spousal abuse or discord. Fennel seeds protect against unquiet spirits. Pine, lupines, bee balm, oak, and acorns are all good for protection spells. Violets work well against bad fortune. Thistles increase bravery. Burn hydrangea bark to break a spell against you. Use peony root to protect children and Saint John's Wort against lightning and fire. Place a wreath made of mugwort over a doorway to protect the inhabitants of the dwelling. Cedar trees protect your property and its inhabitants. Yarrow protects against enemies, particularly jealous ones.

Pentagrams are very effective in protection magick, drawn in the invoking form to protect yourself or another or a place, and in the banishing form to repel and be rid of someone or something. Inscribe the pentagrams, perhaps in the air with your athame or forefinger, while building your white, blue, or black shield. You can inscribe a banishing pentagram on books, tools and objects to protect them. A triskele symbol or a symbol of three intertwined circles or ovals.

There is an old charm sometimes known as a witch's bottle which consists of a small bottle filled with rusty nails, pins, bits of broken glass and broken mirror with jagged edges and then filled with your own urine. This seems really disgusting by modern sensibilities but can be very effective. These are supposed to be buried at the four corners of your property. It is worth noting that I started this charm the summer that my ancestral home partially burned and was sold. I had buried two such bottles at two corners of the property and not finished with the last two. The people that bought the place in the end came from the driveway, which was one of the corners where I had not placed a bottle.

Sea water is useful in protection spells, as are pictures and images of boars, pigs, roosters, bears and lions and other big cats. Bulls and snakes can also be effective. The symbol known as the Eye of Horus. Working protection magick on a Monday is most potent. You can make a protection charm to carry with you using a black or white pouch, perhaps containing an obsidian arrow head, a bit of turquoise, some yarrow, rosemary and sage, an acorn, a picture of a tiger or lion or snake, some salt, a rusty nail, a small mirror (to return to sender) and white and black wax, or any variation of protection correspondences that feel right to you. Create it on a Monday during a waning moon to banish someone or something that is doing you harm or a waxing moon to build your defences, perhaps with the moon in Scorpio or Leo. Use black and white candles and frankincense, myrrh, or patchouli incense, with perhaps pine or violet oil. You may also wish to make use of the large selection of protection powders, oils, incense and candles available commercially. If so cleanse them first and infuse them with your own energy and materials.

Health and Healing

There are so many ailments and so many cures it's hard to know where to begin and what to include. Of course all types of healing magick are meant to augment, rather than replace modern medicine and a doctor's advice. In addition I don't recommend ever ingesting any type of herbal or home remedy without knowing precisely what it is. The herbs listed below are meant, unless otherwise noted, to be used in a spell for healing rather than taken internally.

The colours blue, green and white. The colour red for blood disorders, heart issues, colds and "cold ailments" such as arthritis. The colour blue for fevers and inflammation.

The Goddesses Isis, Gaia, and Diana, and Brid, especially for children's health and well-being.

Agates, especially the lace type, amethysts for pain and afflictions involving alcohol, topaz (any colour, but especially blue), aventurine, carnelian, jade, green jasper, sapphire, and lapis lazuli are all good for general health. In addition, pumice and geodes are good for childbirth, cat's eye for mental health, and bloodstone for anything to do with blood and to stop bleeding and promote health. Diamonds are good for sexual health and flint for headaches, perhaps a good inclusion in a headache pillow. Clear, crystal or smoky quartz could be incorporated into all healing and health spells, charged with magickal intent. Water boiled with a piece of quartz in it and then cooled and drunk is a potent health tonic.

For healing spells you can use balsam fir, eucalyptus, especially for colds and flu, ginger, mullein, sandalwood, violets, cedar boughs, and catnip. Raspberry leaves soaked in ice water can be applied directly to minor burns. Blackcurrants and blackcurrant preserve. A slice of potato or onion can be applied to a bee or wasp sting both to soothe it and to draw out the stinger. A white silken cord knotted around a cedar sprig is a fine healing correspondence. Willow and willow bark is good for spells to ease pain, as are poppies; witch hazel can be used in spells for skin conditions. Mint brewed in a tea and drunk or used in a spell works well for stomach complaints. Lavender for headaches. Birch bark for fever spells, calendula for inflammation, St. John's Wort and lily of the valley aid with depression, as does hyacinth. Chamomile does wonders to soothe and calm both in spells and as a tea. Comfrey leaf helps in spells to restore athletes who have been injured and wish to return to former prowess. Marigold is good for scars, both in spells and in a bath. Sea salt is useful in all types of healing spells.

For a soothing bath try some lavender, chamomile, mint or dandelion. Use juniper, oregano, sage or bay for sore muscles, and basil, pine, parsley, lemon balm and rosemary to feel alert and wakeful. Use a good handful of fresh leaves, about half a handful if dried. Crush them up in your hands and throw them right in the bath or wrap them in a cotton cloth and tie it below the hot tap.

Saturday and the planetary influence of Saturn. Snakes, frogs and toads (but no eye of newt!), horses, falcons, and antlered creatures such as deer. Use a Waxing moon in Aries or Virgo to increase health or a waning moon in Virgo to decrease or banish and illness or disease. Consider for a moment the word "disease." It is literally dis ease. Take this into account when working health and healing magick, especially on oneself. What is a cause of disease or discomfort? How can this be addressed through magick? Also, it is said that a cold is extremely close in symptoms to crying. That is not to say that every time you get a cold there is some terrible thing in your life that is making your body cry, but it worth thinking about and bearing in mind when you do a healing spell. You want to address any underlying conditions or issues and heal the whole, not just the top layer of a problem.

So much health and healing magick is accomplished through visualization and the projection of strength, well-being and appropriate coloured light onto a patient or a poppet of them. Try to visit the sick person if it safe (i.e. you will not spread germs to them and make them sicker) and concentrate on bathing them in a powerful light of blue, for fevers, inflammations, as well as child birth, red for heart and blood problems, or green or white for general healing. You may also want to make a poppet of the person in question, perhaps out of white or green cloth (or you could use blue for a man or pink for a woman) and fill it with cotton and healing herbs and stones, including a charged clear or smoky quartz. You may include finger nail clippings or a bit of hair from the person if it is obtainable and they are okay with it, as well as photographs of the person. Lay the poppet upon your altar, anointed with an oil such as rosemary or a prepared healing oil, while burning green, blue (or red) and white candles and suitable incense, violet, sandalwood, or a prepared type, perhaps on a Saturday with a Virgo moon. Focus your healing energies on the poppet, while chanting "person's name well and whole," about thirty times. Lay your hands on the poppet and pour forth a white healing light and see the person well and happy, up and around again. Consider asking the Lady and Lord's assistance in making this person better. After a moon's turn or when the person is perceptibly better either bury the poppet or take it apart and scatter the contents into a moving body of water.

Justice

I do not have a great deal of correspondences for justice, but I include them because this can be a burning need within us. If we, or someone we love has been wronged we cannot always rely on the justice system to be correct and sometimes we long to do something ourselves. A spell for justice is good remedy to feeling helpless; and this way we ensure that we direct our energy to the right place. Try to use words such as "I seek justice for so and so in the matter of blank" rather than "I want so and so punished." This type of spell can also work in the favour of those wrongfully imprisoned or persecuted.

The colours blue, orange or purple. Also, black for return to sender. Wear blue to court if possible, and some orange where it doesn't show. This is isn't exactly a correspondence, but if you have to go to court it helps to listen carefully, be respectful and try very hard not to exclaim or cry out.

The Goddesses Justica, Athene or Minerva, Demeter or Ceres, Irene, Maat, Medusa, Brigantia for triumph, and Nemesis for help against criminals. The numbers 4, 16, and 21.

Dragon's blood ink and incense, and even soap if you can find it. Obsidian, silver, slate, jet, amethyst, aragonite, and some pieces of jasper. Bloodstones, carnelians, marble, amazonite, and sardonyx are also useful stones in justice spells. Pussy willows, oak and acorns. Lavender against abuse. Juniper berries and foliage, as well as St. John's wort, hickory wood, marigolds, mullein, vervain leaves, carnations, galangal root, elm bark, anise and cinnamon. Dirt from a court house or jail. Symbols or pictographs of a scale or those depicting a balance. Snakes, lions, ladybugs, sharks, and again, wolves. A wolf pack is very fair and just. Frankincense incense and oil are good, and musk works well also.

Work justice magick on a Wednesday or Sunday, during a waxing moon to increase the power of the truth coming out or a waning moon to diminish the wrong doing. Use a moon in Pisces for anything to do with the police, or a moon in Sagittarius or

Libra for general justice.

Beauty/Looking good

This is another subject on which my correspondence list is not huge but it is a fun one. Use beauty correspondences along with a glamour spell or enchanted personal care items. Remember also to drink lots of water, get as much sleep as you can and eat a balanced diet.

The colours yellow, orange and gold. The numbers 6, 12, 13 and 18.

The Goddesses Branwen, Freyja, Hathor, Idhunn, Niamh, and Arianrhod.

Oatmeal and oats. Try using facial products that contain oatmeal extract or even an empowered mask of oatmeal itself. Cedar, asters, morning glories and delphiniums. Sweet peas, and crushed sweet pea flowers steeped in ice water and splashed on the face. Rose water and rose petals, jasmine, magnolia, ivy, and mistletoe. Peonies and peony petals are useful in beauty magick. Peas, apples and apple wood, lemon peel, sunflowers, cloves, myrtle, avocado, flax, ginseng, dill, bayberry, as well as yellow iris and nasturtiums.

Iron pyrite, turquoise, jade, milky, rose, and crystal quartz. As well, cat's eye, jasper, peridot, zircon, and some say moonstone. Purple quartz if you can find it. Diamonds and diamond shapes. Mirrors, especially mirrors that you cast a spell over to see the beauty in yourself reflected on the outside.

Dolphins, unicorns, swans, and oddly, sheep and mice. A braid of orange and yellow silk. Waxing crescent moon symbols, and plain (that is, not pentagrams) five pointed stars. Prepared beauty oil, lemon, jasmine, or magnolia oil.

Work beauty magick on a Thursday, during a waxing moon to increase good looks and a waning moon to decrease anything you would be rid of. Use a Taurus, Leo, Libra or Aquarius moon phase. The main thing to remember is the better you feel you look the better you will look because confidence really makes you look better. A good beauty spell will make you feel wonderful about your looks and that will shine through and make you look spectacular.

Weather

It should go without saying that one must be very careful with weather magick. It can grow out of control so easily and do harm. Also, it is not always possible to foresee all the implications changing or affecting the weather can have, so it is important to be cautious and hone your intent carefully.

The colours blue, gray, brown and white. The Goddesses Aine, Nut, Cailleach Bheur, and sometimes Diana.

You can burn ferns, heather, or bracken to cause rain. It is much better to do this outdoors on an open lawn than indoors. Also you can burn a blue or gray candle in front of you with the flame at eye level and stare into it chanting "come rain come rain come rain come rain" for about 15 minutes and extinguish the flame with a sharp hand clap.

You can make a loose knot in a blue, tan, or silver cord and blow through the loop gently as you tighten the knot, then make a second and a third knot blowing harder and harder before tightening each one. When the knots are unbound in order they raise a breeze, a wind and a gale. Strong visualization should accompany both the knotting and the unknotting. There is even an old Finnish woodcut of a wise man selling such a knotted charm to a sailor who fears becoming becalmed at sea. Another method of raising a wind is to dip a bit of white cotton in a fast moving body of water and then beat it briskly three times against a rock while visualizing a strong wind. Also, you can stand outside at dawn and whistle three sharp blasts while facing the direction you wish the wind to come from. Daffodils and large feathers also work well in magick to raise a wind, as do saffron and broom.

Pictures or pictographs or figures of cranes, herons and fish. Raven images work well to help raise a storm and goat images help in protection against storms. Symbols of storm clouds, lightning bolts, falling rain and so on can be very useful, especially when made by hand. An image of three spirals arranged in a triangle with a jagged lightning bolt descending for storms. A bottle of water to splash about and toss in the air can help call rain in a base form of sympathetic magick. Chalcedony, smoky quartz, calcite, pearls, peridot, and aquamarine are all useful in general weather magick, although pearls should be cleansed carefully before use with care paid to thanking the creature who died to harvest them. Dogwood, hazel, and white roses are also helpful for all types of weather work. For rain use pansies, toadstools, and try tossing rice in the air. The numbers 3, 10, 15. Spiders are good; I usually use pictures of them and don't recommend squishing them to cause rain, although many in my family swear by this method. Instead of burning ferns or heather they may be used upon the altar or in the Circle to affect the weather.

In addition, there are some signs that portend certain weather conditions. Although they are not actual correspondences they are interesting to look for: Red sky at night, sailors delight (fair weather the next day). Red sky at morning, sailor take warning, (stormy unsettled conditions this day). Clouds like wool or mare tails, and evening rainbows suggest fair weather, twinkling stars, cows lying down, crows fussing, and frogs croaking mean rain. Seeing the underside of the leaves during a wind gust means a storm coming, as well as bees staying in their hives, pale sunrises and dogs rolling. Ducks flapping and herons flying high above the clouds as well as rustling leaves and floating thistledown in the air mean wind.

We used to do a rain dance when it was dry, but it wasn't very formal, just a lot of spinning, jumping and clapping, calling for rain. It had mixed results but burned off a lot of excess energy and tension.

Prosperity

Prosperity suggests obviously money and wealth, but it is not about having large cash injections appear out of thin air. This type of magick is mostly about having what you need, unless you specify in your spell that you want more than that. It's a good idea when working prosperity magick to write down what your needs are, perhaps with green ink, and have the list on your altar while you work your spell.

The colours green, silver, and gold are useful for prosperity, as are the numbers 4, 16, and 28. Green ink and candles are especially helpful, as are gold and silver candles and ink. The Goddesses Danu, Hathor, Anu, Nerthus, and especially Epona. The green man or the God Pan. The planet Jupiter, juniper sprigs, pine, ficus, sweet woodruff, alfalfa, allspice, oak, onions, maple, poplars, mint, ferns, grapes, poppies, dock, snapdragons, zinnias, and all types of moss are good bets for money and prosperity magick. Also, kelp, coltsfoot, nutmeg, basil, marjoram, and especially pine. Adventurine, coal, turquoise, malachite, tiger's eye, emeralds, rubies, bloodstones, topaz, green slate, lodestones, peridots, green tourmalines, and especially jade. Any green coloured stones or stones with silver or gold coloured specks.

Bears, buffalo, stags, unicorns, toads, fish and elephants. Equal armed crosses. Talc and salt.

Bayberry candles, sandalwood or frankincense incense, pine oil, sesame seeds and oil. Braids of green, gold, and silver ribbons or cords. Cash and pound symbols, as well as invoking pentagrams to grow your wealth. Patchouli oil, soap, and incense. Make a "dish garden" of moss in a green or gold coloured shallow bowl, including a mirror and enchant it for prosperity. Care for it well and see your financial well being improve. Give away slightly more than you comfortably can to charity or relatives (I am not saying break the bank, but if you were going to give $10, give $12). Healthy plants in your home and using all four elements of your stove help with money magick, as do gnomes, and Earth elementals.

Work prosperity magick on a Tuesday or Thursday with a waxing moon in Taurus, Virgo, Capricorn or Leo to increase wealth and a waning moon in Virgo or Capricorn to reduce debts.

Empower your bank card or cheque book, as well as coins or a piggy bank to grow your money, pick up even pennies off the ground, and store cash in your Book of Shadows at the place where you have recorded your prosperity spell. Like attracts like.

Spirituality

Spirituality magick can be worked to find an animal spirit guide, to grow closer to the Goddess and God and interpret what they might be saying to you, and to find a rich new level to your life.

Those with a full spiritual side to their lives are often happier and more fulfilled.

The colours purple, silver, and to a lesser extent, blue and white. White, purple, and silver cords in a braid and purple and silver candles. Also, the colour indigo is helpful to some.

The Goddesses Danu, Nephthys, Ningal, Baat, Gaia, Bast, Blodeuwedd, Cerridwen, the Morrigan, and any Goddess and God you feel a special association with, as well as Brid, for learning about the great mysteries and spiritual matters.

African violets, sweetgrass, gardenia, myrrh, aloe, tobacco, bay, thyme, peach, peppermint, celery, acacia, calendula, lily of the valley, foxglove, anise, lemon balm, eyebright herb, iris, sage, thistle, and wintergreen are all helpful in magick to improve or strengthen your spirituality. In spirit animal magick use wintergreen, sage, sweetgrass, iris, foxglove, thyme and thistle especially. In terms of stones, purple lapidolite, aquamarine, coral (not taken from a living reef!), amethysts, pink tourmalines, citrine, lapis, geodes, calcite, sugilite, and diamonds are all good. For some, rainbow moonstone works well (try to handle a piece and see how it makes you feel. Spiritual?). Your own birthstone may be helpful.

Your own pet can be a tremendous help with your spiritual development. Try to include them and have them present during your spells or meditations on this subject, as long as they are not too excitable. In addition, bees, blackbirds, hedgehogs, seagulls, cranes, griffins, spiders, crows, cobras and especially owls can be helpful if they are used in picture or figurine form. Pictures of a human figure with spirals or pentagrams drawn on their forehead or "third eye," perhaps you could use a picture of yourself for this. The moon. Listening to lapping waves and smelling (perhaps in the form of incense) lavender or sweetgrass. Sage and frankincense incense. Lavender or peppermint oil. The presence of your own spirit or totem animal if you are already familiar with them. The numbers 1, 6, 11, 18. Work spirituality magick on a Monday or Sunday, with the moon in Pisces if at all possible, or perhaps with the moon in the sign it was in at your birth. For spiritual spell correspondences it helps to use your intuition and look for things which make you feel open, mystical, and ready to reach a higher level.

Luck

Here we are looking at correspondences to aid achieving good luck. You may wish to do a good luck spell before a test, job interview, presentation, doctor's visit, date, or the like. Some people like to empower a token of some kind during a luck spell and carry it with them always, a small stone, medal, key or coin works well for this.

The colour green especially, and also yellow and silver. Green candles, cords and ink, as well as silver or yellow ink on green paper.

The Goddesses Freya, Cerridwen, Gefion and the Moerae. Also the God Bacchus.

Daffodils, tulips, trilliums, willow twigs, ash leaves, basil, mustard seeds, parsley, black-eyed susans, tonka beans, peony, cinnamon, anise, carnation petals, and of course, four leaf clovers and clover in general. Black walnut wood, bark, twigs and black walnuts themselves are very lucky. Sweet woodruff is good for luck in business, as are pussy willow boughs. Also bluebells, aloe, bamboo, holly, heather, hazel, gentians, straw, and pomegranates. Pine wood and pine cones. Agates, especially moss or lace agates and something called Botswana agate. Cobalt blue and green obsidian, as well as alexandrite, lapidolite, apache tears, adventurine, cat's eye, jade, amber, and chalcedony. Copper is lucky, as are black cats and dogs, most other cats, quail, and swallows, cardinals, toads, and rabbits. I do not believe that rabbit's feet are lucky however, since I don't see how the death of one creature can bring another good fortune. It might be different if you hunt the rabbit yourself, take it respectfully and eat the meat. Saying "lucky rabbits foot," first thing on the first of every month is lucky, as is seeing a cardinal in a birch tree, but neither of those are spell correspondences, I just mention them for fun.

The numbers 7, 11, and 13. Pine incense and oil, as well as dragon's blood, and prepared luck oils and incenses. Dice, jacks from decks of playing cards, hammers, and triquetras or symbols of three interlocked circles or ovals. Do luck magick on a Wednesday with a waxing moon in Gemini if you can. NOTE: There are hundreds of commercially available luck tokens and these are fine to use, but it is a good idea to empower them and imbue them with your special energy during a good luck spell.

Travel

What kind of travel spell are you going to be doing? Well, one to go travelling. My sister does these quite a bit with great success. At first it seems impossible, her husband says he can't get away this year; the school holiday is at an inconvenient time or the travel fund is low, but she works away at it, usually with pictures of the place she'd like to visit and somehow the money shows up and everything gets resolved and off they go. The other type of travel spell that you may wish to do is for safe travelling, these are especially good for nervous flyers.

The colours blue, white and orange. The Goddesses Brigantia, Epona, Freyja, Rhiannon and Hina.

Poplar and tarragon for success in going on a trip, as well as orange zircon, chalcedony, and sugar cubes. Use items from the place you'd like to travel to, perhaps obtained on a previous trip, or pictures taken there. For safety on a trip carry a small pebble from home or a leopard agate or any spotted stone. St. John's wort and lilac blossoms work for safe travel as well. Migratory birds, horses, and centaurs will help you to get a trip together and images of snakes, gazelles, and turtles can help with safe travel. Place a dusting of soil from home in your shoes to travel safely and a dusting of sand or soil from your destination to return there again. Carry mugwort to prevent jet lag and travelling fatigue and use mugwort in a spell to go on a trip. Geodes help with travel plans and travel safety. Brass, silk and the planet Mercury help in spells to travel and tin helps with travel safety spells. Pictures of the place you'd like to visit or the type of place are good to use in a spell to get you there and pictures of home are for a safe return. Use sunflower or dragon's blood oil and sandalwood or lilac incense to make travel happen, and patchouli oil and incense for safe travel. You may combine the spell to go on a trip with the spell to travel safely, but I prefer to do them separately. Do a spell to be able to travel on a Sunday with a waxing moon in Sagittarius, and a spell for safe travel on a Wednesday with a waning moon in Sagittarius. The sign of Sagittarius helps with all things related to travel. Pictographs of the sign, booking or travelling when the sun or moon is in Sagittarius, and dealing with people of this sign can be extremely useful in anything travel related.

Above all, keep in mind that all correspondences are aids to your own focus. It is wonderful to obtain two or three or ten correspondences for each spell but if you cannot get the perfect incense or the best oil your magick will not fall apart! The power and energy for manifestation comes primarily from within you. The energies present in correct correspondences are beneficial and help you direct your intention but you have the ability to change your own reality. By all means try to collect and create the perfect correspondences but don't worry if there are some you can't find. Try drawing images of animals and symbols yourself and making braids out coloured cords and ribbons by hand. Imbue as much of your own personal energy into each item by handling it and focusing your intent on it and the magick will be created regardless of whether you have managed to get violet incense or dried mullein. Blessed be!

10: A WITCH'S SPELLS

Of all the ideas the general population has about witches and witchcraft, the one that even the most casual layperson has is that witches cast spells. Fantastic spells that make a person fly through the air, turn into an animal, become completely invisible or look completely different have been told of in folktales and fables throughout history and re-occur in today's pop culture with the stories of Harry Potter and his friends and others. The image of a terrifying hag muttering over a steaming cauldron filled with things like eye of newt and tail of dog is one held among school children even in this modern world, as it has been for many centuries. But what of real witches and the spells they work? Do spells really work? How do they work? Can you actually become invisible? Change your appearance into something else totally? Fly? Well, in a way. There are spells that make you so unnoticeable you seem to disappear, spells that let you take the essence of an animal into yourself, and carry it with you, for confidence and power, and through astral travel you can feel as though you are flying, and indeed visit other places far away in your mind. You can find old recipes for witches flying ointments that contain things like hashish and belladonna, and rubbing them on your body may make you feel as though you are flying, but this is not recommended. There are love potions that truly turn a person's head, and money spells that have really worked for my family and me. A properly cast spell can give you the power to change your life and anything in it.

How does it work? Where does the power come from? There are several schools of thought on this. Some believe that the power comes from the intervention of spirits and ghosts, that when you cast a spell you are getting their attention and asking for them to make changes in your world. Others believe that the power of magick comes from dealing correctly with the four elements, fire, air, water and earth. Even in my tradition there are several different beliefs on the source of the power that makes a spell work. Some believe that all the power comes from within you. That it is created by your subconscious mind and correspondences and spell formats merely send a message to the subconscious, which in turn directs the conscious mind on what to do to create the desired effect through your own force of will. The more spells that are performed and the more studying and learning you do the more your subconscious will recognize the messages you are sending it. Visualization and other energy raising methods add a wallop of weight to the message you are sending yourself. Others believe that there is a force inherent to Earth that is not yet detectable to science but is nevertheless very real. Arguments for this belief include the fact that one hundred years ago scientists were unable to detect, measure, or quantify many of the energies and forces they can today. New discoveries are happening all the time that teach us amazing things about our universe that we had no idea about before. Quantum mechanics, a fascinating subject in its own right has thrown much of what we thought we knew about matter and energy out of the window. It is being suggested that all things in our galaxy are connected and the same at a sub-molecular level, and thus one should be able to manifest anything they choose, as everything is fundamentally the same (although the how of this is still somewhat unclear, spells are one way to attempt this manifestation). Alchemy for the 21st century! But getting back to the power source of magick, and an undetectable force present in our world, it is thought that anyone can tap into it with the right aids and this has been recognized by cultures all over the world. We do not have a word for this power in the English language, but many others do, to the ancient Egyptians it was haka, and the name that is known to many gamers today is mana. Correspondences and other spell components resonate with a frequency that helps to harness this power and put it at your disposal. While doing a spell you collect some of the energy that is present everywhere, and in all living things, and direct it where you will.

Some in my tradition hold to a combination of these two beliefs: That you utilize a powerful energy present naturally in our world and a tremendous power latent in your own subconscious to make a spell work. What you believe will have to be your own decision. What feels correct or makes sense to you. For some, it is like many things in life: you don't need to understand how a computer or telephone works to use one and get the full benefit of it.

So now we have an idea about the basis of the power that makes a spell work we should talk about what a spell *is*. Generally, when we think of a spell we think of the aforementioned hag and cauldron, or if we are more enlightened we think of Wiccans in white robes chanting over white candles (which is certainly a valid and good image). I was taught however, that there are many, many kinds of spells. Many powerful spells dictate that you gather your correspondences and ingredients, choose your timing, ritually prepare, set up your altar and do a spell. Yet there are other types of spells too. A bath can be a spell. Washing your hair can be a spell. Making a scrapbook or photo album can be a spell. A bonfire or candle can be a spell. Giving someone a gift or singing a song can be a spell. A walk in the woods, a fishing trip, or any mundane action can be a spell. What turns an everyday action or even a series of potent magickal ingredients and special words into a spell is you. While one aunt might say that the power comes from your own mind alone, and another might scoff and say the power is present everywhere and needs to be made productive both would certainly agree that neither type of power is good for anything without you. Your desire, your intention, your will, your focus, concentration and direction.

In order to do any type of spell at all you need to have an intention, commonly referred to as an intent or magickal intent. This is the first seed of the magick. The intent usually springs up from a need, a lack, a problem or a desire. For example your roof leaks, your savings account is empty and you need money to fix it, or you feel lonely and you desire to be more confident in meeting new people so you can have more friends. Your intents in these cases would be money and confidence. But it is important to refine the intent and be totally aware of it going in. Instead of just "money", it would be "enough money to fix the roof that comes to me from somewhere I haven't thought of but is reasonably available to me" (as in, your crazy friend from high school doesn't show up with a bag of stolen twenties to hide for him). Or instead of just "confidence," it would be better to think of something like "I want to be more confident when I meet new people, be less nervous, so the real me shines out and I can make new friends." Before anything else try to get a handle on what you really need or want and make it specific. Try to fully picture the outcome as you would have it in full detail ahead of even preparing for the spell. See yourself smiling up at a brand new roof or surrounded by a laughing group of people just like you who you can count on and be real with. The more you fix your intent in your mind going in the better your spell will work.

Next choose the type of spell. This can be tough, as there are thousands out there. Some are based on ancient Egyptian and Greek formulas, some are full of expensive and tricky to obtain materials and complicated instructions, some depend on specific timing or locations; some are as simple as burning a candle and saying a few words. There are tons of fabulous spell books for sale today, free spells on the Internet, spell kits from witchcraft supply outlets, and then there are spells you make yourself. It's usually agreed by magickal people that spells of your own devising are the most potent. They come from your own heart, are specifically tailored to your exact needs and come into being as a product of your own will, all mighty effective components. Generally it is also accepted that spells and words that have been repeated hundreds or thousands of times by many people over long periods of time to achieve the same results are real powerhouses as well. Old spells are wonderful too because they were created by those more in tune with the natural world, and its rhythms and cycles. Another thing to consider is whether you want to sit down and do a spell and have it done, or you want something more subtle, something you work at a little every day. Using the examples above you might want to do a spell and have it out there in the universe to get your roof fixed as soon as possible, but to improve your confidence and outlook you might want something that changes gradually, improves with time, something which you add to again and again. Again it's important to note that what exactly constitutes a spell is dependent on you. For growing self confidence you might start with a candle spell, gazing into a mirror and seeing yourself as you want others to see you, and then for weeks afterward you might, for example have a little mantra that you repeat every day as you dress and get ready, something like "As I step into my pants I am braver, with each button I button I have more courage. With each stroke of the comb I am less nervous. When I put on my shoes I am sure of my place in the world." It sounds a little silly maybe, but these kinds of positive cues are widely recognized in fields outside of magick, such as psychotherapy.

You will also want to have a clear idea in your head whether the spell you are going to do is projective in that it sends something out, like the need for money for a new roof, or receptive in that it brings something into you, like self confidence.

Once you have an intent and a specific spell in mind you can begin to gather your correspondences and ingredients. If you are using a spell that you have found it will dictate what you need. For a spell you make yourself you choices are broad. Choose one or three or ten correspondences from *A Witch's Spell Correspondences*, choose different coloured candles, cords and/or cloth from *A Witch's Colour Wheel*, choose a moon sign and phase from *A Witch's Moon*. In addition choose things that evoke your intent. A picture of a new roof or the type of person you want in your life or a new car and so on. An item from a place you wish to go or from a person you wish to affect. A business card or printed pages from the website of the company you want to work for. A clock to have more time for something, a deck of cards for luck with gaming. A personal good luck token or a special outfit to wear. Pens with different coloured inks, handmade or unique paper, or a quill and ink. Anything that makes the spell closer to the place, person, action or desire of your intent will help to focus the energies. One of the fundamental principles of magick in my tradition is that like attracts like.

Once you have assembled everything you need and chosen your timing, be it a moon phase, (believed to have the most effect on the outcome,) moon sign, day of the week, a planetary reference or any combination of those, you will want to prepare yourself to work magick. Ritual preparation is outlined in *A Witch's Body of Ritual*, but there are other considerations. First of all you will want to decide if a Circle is necessary or will be beneficial. It is a tremendous aid to focus, which is the foundation of any successful spell, but it is not always practical. You will want to spend some time either in meditation simply breathing deeply and becoming calm, alert, and focused. Then you will have to make a final decision on how you want to raise the energy needed as the engine of the spell. You can decide this ahead of time, of course, and if you are using sex magick with a partner (see *A Witch's Sex Magick*) you will need to have them there. But sometimes at the last minute you will decide another method is better and it is usually a good idea to follow these little "hunches," in this and all things to do with magick and witchcraft.

There are loads of ways to raise energy: dancing, chanting, drumming, or some combination of those, visualization, sexual tension, exercise, communicating with the deities, tapping into the mystical Oneness of everything in the universe (a technique that may take years to perfect), controlled breathing, self-hypnosis, as well as blood control, fasting, delirium, drugs, drinking, scourging, hot wax dripping and ritualized cutting (which are NOT recommended, but nevertheless are out there), and others too. The friendliest so to speak or the best to attempt at first are dancing, drumming, chanting, visualization and sexual self-stimulation. Dancing has been mentioned as a method for energy raising throughout the history of magick. Even people like me for whom dancing is difficult can utilize it to lower inhibitions, free themselves, induce different states of consciousness necessary to create magick and raise a lot of good energy. Just moving, throwing your arms up, whirling, and jumping up and down will do it, we are not talking about the fox trot here. Drumming in a steady rhythm that builds to a culmination works well also. Chanting is the same: rhythmic, and building to a height, at which point the energy is sent outwards toward a goal or in some cases drawn into you to effect a change within.

Some measure of visualization is important for every spell. When you are forming your intent you want to visualize the outcome that you are working towards and it is a good idea to do this as you work on a spell and while you send the energy out. Visualizing is a technique that should be honed. Practise some visualization ahead of time. Seat yourself comfortably and close your eyes. Now try to remember every detail of the room you are in. The pieces of furniture, and where they are in relation to each other. The colour and texture of the ceiling, the location and size of the windows, all the sundry items on a table. How much can you picture and how clearly can you picture it? This is a good starting point, and you can try doing it once a week or so until you can do it in all sorts of places, not just your own home. Next you can try picturing other places, places you have been or places you would like to go. See and feel them, the sounds, the smells, the colours. Later, as you feel you are gaining proficiency you can work on situations, seeing yourself with a lover, happily entwined, seeing yourself in a store buying what you want; seeing yourself surrounded by a group of people having a blast. These scenes should be completely detailed, again, with smells, sounds, and in three dimensions.

Visualization for energy raising should start with a perfectly realized scene that matches your spells intent and then cycle through other scenes. If you are searching for a mate for example, see and feel yourself with them, walking down the street holding hands, laughing in a restaurant, on a plane together flying to an exotic destination, crying out in passion in a bed, standing at an altar saying vows. Go through each scene in perfect clarity, taking as much time as needed to focus on it, and then go through them all again and again, speeding up until the images are almost flashing through your mind, a giggle, a smile, a gasp of pleasure, a sunlit beach, arms tight around you. When they are almost a blur you can send the energy out. You will get a sense of this timing with practise. Done right, with intense focus and concentration visualization can be an extremely powerful aid to a spell.

Some found spells will have a line in them that says "picture the outcome you desire in your mind," or "Focus on the spell manifesting," which will give you a set time to do visualization during the spell. Many spells do not have anything like this, or indeed, anything about energy raising of any kind. You will have to decide on the timing based on the found spell. The spell may be something like "throw salt in a fire and then chant such and such." So when do you raise the energy? Like so much in witchcraft the choice is yours. The answer is, whenever you think it is best. Before throwing the salt in the fire. After throwing the salt in the fire, but before chanting the incantation (that would be my choice in this case) or after doing both. Each spell is different and has a different tempo of its own so there is no hard and fast rule. What is important is that you do raise some energy and send it out at some point during the spell work. The energy you raise and send combined with your focus, concentration and belief is the legs and body of your spell, no matter what correspondences or trappings are used.

Belief is another important matter for spells. You really have to believe that what you're doing can work, will work, and is already working. There is a saying in magick that goes 'Believe you have it and you have it.' Some go so far as to say that spells and magick do nothing more than alter your own perception of reality. I can see how this could be in true in a lot of situations except in prosperity magick. I haven't quite wrapped my head around how you can perceive that your bank balance is higher than it was if it isn't. However, belief is intrinsic to a spells success, even down to the wording of a spell: try to change a found spell's wording or write your own wording to make it reflect the present tense. We *are* happy together and in love. I *have* enough money to cover the rent. I *have* a job at blank.

What about all these correspondences you have painstakingly collected and assembled? Now you have them, what do you *do* with them? Well, some found spells will tell you what to do with them. In this case they are ingredients for a potion or pouch or poppet or are to be buried, burned, or tossed into a moving body of water and the like. In the case of your own spells they could be used the same way; stuffed into a pouch that you will keep under your pillow or in your pocket, placed in a box together and put away so they can keep working together even after you have finished performing your spell, placed somewhere wild so they will dissolve, decay, or return to nature as your spell works. But during the spell they generally sit on the altar or are arrayed around you. There, they lend their unique energies and powers to the work you are doing. You may wish to imbue them with the four elements by smoking them with incense, sprinkling them with salt and water and running them through, or above, a candles flame. You may wish to hold them tightly in your hands or have them on your lap as you raise and send your energy. You may wish to dedicate each item to the Lord and Lady and then leave them outside for them as a token of thanks knowing that it will make your spell that much more powerful. Even if you should throw them away afterward they will lend their energies to the work as you do it, and help corral your focus to where it needs to be.

The ethics of a witch were discussed in *A Witch's World*, but here is an example of an ethical consideration for a spell. My better half comes to me and says he has a bet on a football team called the Colts. Can I do something to make the Ravens (the other team) lose? Well, probably yes. Curses and hexes are easy to find, and offer a seductive amount of power. But they are really not a good idea. Sending out that type of malevolent energy, whether you believe that a deity is keeping score, or not, is just not wise. Call it karma or the threefold law or whatever you like but what you give is what you get, so what you want to get is what you should spend your time on. Instead of doing something to make the Ravens lose, I concentrated instead on good luck and good fortune for the Colts and prosperity for us (it worked out beautifully, by the way). Many conundrums can be flipped this way. Instead of misfortune for someone who is trying to steal your credit at work concentrate on shining yourself and getting noticed for your achievements or having opportunities come your way. Instead of trying to be rid of someone who you think is after your boy or girlfriend try a spell to turn them into your friend or one to make yourself irresistible.

The only time you should actively work against someone with magick is if they are doing real harm to you or another. In this case try a binding or a banishing. A binding can be accomplished by wrapping a photograph or image of them in mostly black with a little bit of white ribbon or tape and visualizing them neutralized and powerless over those they would harm during a Circle, then burying the image, still wrapped in black and white. You can write a banishing spell and perform it during the waning moon, as well as visualizing them swept out of your life (or the life of the one they are hurting) while you sweep, wash, or stir anything counter clockwise. Be sure when you form your intent that it is clear that what you are doing is not malicious, it is to protect yourself or another, or to keep someone from having power over you or another.

In terms of writing wordings for spells you make yourself you can be as creative as you like or feel comfortable with. If you are musically inclined you could write a song, complete with music and lyrics if you choose. Your wording could be a poem or a chant. Keep in mind that you want it to have a rhythm that makes it easy to say and repeat. Repetition is a good thing in spell wordings, as is rhyme. As long as what you are saying clearly encapsulates your intent, is definite and comes from your heart you cannot go far wrong. Many people these days like to add something like "For the good of all," or "As long as no harm comes to any person, or place or thing." These kinds of mystical "get out of jail free cards," are benign, but remember if your intent is harmful, adding something like this does not change it. Don't be afraid of magick. Your spell can have unintended consequences, yes, but if your intent is carefully thought out, your outcome clearly visualized and your desire is not hurtful, it will be alright. Do make sure to think of possible ramifications of what you are casting, and be responsible for the implications of your actions. The golden rule is in play here: "Do onto others as you would have them do unto you." For spell wordings people often like to incorporate somewhat archaic terminology. They say 'thee' instead of 'you,' and so on. For some this evokes a bygone era when magick was everywhere and practitioners were highly respected. For others it makes a spell more "real." Occasionally a found spell will use archaic words. Whether you update them or keep them for the "feel," is up to you.   Certainly the old aunts used a lot of archaic words and phrases by modern standards!

How long will a spell take to work? A found spell will often tell you how long it should be before you can expect results, and if not the general rule is one or three turns of the moon. So if it is March and the moon is in its second quarter you can usually expect results when the moon is in its second quarter in April, or in its second quarter in June. For your own spells you can put a time on them, say a moon's turning. You will no doubt want to do this is if time is important, as in the case of the new roof. Resist the urge to add something like "right away," or anything else ambiguous in your wording though. Instead try something like "I have the money for the roof, it is March 15th" (a date about a month in the future).

Why do spells sometimes fail? Or turn out differently than you expected? There are lots of reasons, but don't be discouraged. As with anything you get better at it with practise. Sometimes the focus or concentration isn't strong enough, or enough energy or power wasn't raised, or it leeched away before you could send it. Maybe you got ground wormwood and you thought it was orris root. Maybe the timing was wrong or the moon was void of course, or Mercury was retrograde. Maybe there is an important reason why it didn't work out that you can't see right now. One thing to remember is not to talk about your spell to too many people, or anyone at all except maybe a partner or very close loved one. Other people's disbelief or scepticism can colour a spell and make it lose potency faster than a deflated balloon. Even your own doubt can ruin a spell. You have to believe it will work in order for it to work. So if you tell someone and they say "Oh that'll never work," and you think to yourself 'Oh they're right that will never work, it was a stupid thing to do,' then the spell can fall apart. It is better to, if not completely forget about the spell (which is probably impossible), put it out of your mind as much as you can, unless it is an ongoing spell or a pouch or poppet that you continually add more energy too.

A word we are hearing a lot these days is "manifestation." It relates to new discoveries in Quantum Mechanics, and has become popular on the talk show circuit as well. But long before it was daytime television fodder it was a concept in witchcraft and magick. It relates to having something come about, happen, or become reality as a result of your magick. Energy raising through visualization and other means during a spell and visualization of your intent can lead to its manifestation. In addition, even the way you live your life can lead to manifestation. If you are constantly in a funk, dour, unhappy, and believe you are unworthy of life's riches, then chances are you will be. But, conversely if you are upbeat, actively try to remain optimistic, and open yourself to all the possibilities out there for you, you will manifest a better life for yourself. Manifestation can come from all of our thoughts and actions, not just spells. Try to think that you deserve what you want, that you are already on the way to getting what you want, and try not to dwell on things that could go wrong. This will help tremendously with spell work and life in general.

Substitutions of spell ingredients and correspondences are tricky as everything has an inherent energy. Sometimes you can find a proper substitute for what you need, but more often than not you can't. In the case of spell ingredients it may be better to leave the item out altogether or rework the spell entirely. In general, if the spell you want to use contains something you cannot get you may be better off to use an alternative spell. However, even the most exotic spell ingredients such as foreign plants or rare stones can be ordered over the Internet if you are determined to stick with a certain spell.

A Basic Pouch Spell

Items:

Natural fabric in a colour appropriate to your working, or white.

Needle and thread in an appropriate colour.

A white candle or other colour appropriate to the working.

Herbs, stones, photos, hand drawn pictures or symbols and other small items that evoke your intent.

Cotton balls or baby powder to fill out the pouch.

An oil that is appropriate to the spell's intent.

A chalice of spring water, a bowl of salt, and an incense that correlates to your intent.

Your athame or wand (if you don't have either you can use the pointer finger of your power hand),

Think out and form your intent carefully. Choose a moon

phase that suits your spell, such as waxing quarter for a prosperity spell, and perhaps a moon sign and day of the week that work as well. Cut the fabric into two squares that are the size of the pouch you want, usually about 5 inches by 5 inches. Write a wording that encapsulates your intention, using rhythm and rhyme if possible. Ritually prepare as described in *A Witch's Body of Ritual*, by cleansing and purifying yourself and the area, cast a Circle as described in *A Witch's Circle*, if possible. In this case after the Circle is cast bring the elemental representations back to the altar with you. Have some natural food and drink on hand to ground. Sit comfortably before the altar and sew up three sides of the pouch, visualizing your intent all the while, and perhaps humming a tune that ramps up your energy or repeating a mantra such as "prosperity in the new business," or "a happier love life," with every stitch. Leave the fourth side of the pouch open and turn it inside out so the stitching is on the inside. Circle your wand, athame, or finger clockwise over the assembled items on the altar about twenty times. Now, imbue each item before placing it into the pouch with the four elements; sprinkle it with chalice water and salt, hold it in the incense smoke and above the candle flame as close as possible. Drip a few drops of oil into the pouch. All the while visualize your intent, really concentrating on it. Repeat a mantra if desired. Even the cotton batting or other "filler" material should be imbued. Set the pouch on the altar and raise energy. Dance around the altar, throwing your arms to the sky and clapping your hands. Chant while throwing your arms up and periodically touching the bundle. Raise sexual energy with the pouch on you or between you and your partner. Hold it to your genitals, heart, and forehead as you raise energy through visualization, or use another any other method that you feel is best. At the moment that you sense the energy is at its peak place both hands on the pouch and feel the energy pouring into it. Now slowly and deliberately sew up the fourth side, still visualizing your outcome with all your focus. Circle your athame or wand over the bundle clockwise, filling it with power. Imbue the finished pouch with the elements, saying the wording you have prewritten; something like 'Our new venture is perfect and strong; we have timed the market and know we are not wrong. Matters that we thought hard are easy; our work is fun, rewarding and breezy. We are very happy and rich, magick power flows through this witch.' Repeat your wording as you imbue the pouch with each element. When you are finished once again place the pouch on the altar and rest both hands lightly on it, feeling any leftover energy flowing into it while visualizing your outcome. Anoint the pouch lightly with the oil, just a few drops. Then ground and close the Circle as described in *A Witch's Circle*. Keep the pouch with you, in a pocket or purse or under your pillow until your spell works. If you feel it is getting off track take the pouch out, anoint it again and imbue it with the elements again; if necessary raise more energy and pour it into the pouch. In between times of handling the pouch, try not to think of it or talk to anyone about it.

When the spell has worked to your satisfaction bury the pouch whole in a place where it will not be disturbed or drop it into a body of water saying a short thank you to the deities, or if you prefer, to the universe.

A Basic Candle Spell

Items:

A fat pillar candle in a colour appropriate to your intent.

An oil suitable for your intent.

Dried herbs that suit.

A stone or crystal appropriate to your spell.

Two straight pins.

Once again, form and perfect your intent and choose a moon phase, as well as perhaps a moon sign and day of the week. Write a short wording or chant. Prepare and cast a Circle if it is practical. Sit before the altar and breathe deeply, focusing on your intent. Hold the candle; roll it between your hands, squeeze it, pour your intent into it. Perhaps carve appropriate symbols into it with one of the pins, or just an invoking or banishing pentagram as the need dictates. Now anoint the candle with the oil, rubbing a light coat up from the centre to the top and down from the centre to the base. Stick the two pins in to the candle on opposite sides at the centre. Sprinkle the dried herbs around the candles base and set the crystal in front of it, touching the candle. Light the candle and say your wording; something like 'By the power within in me our love increases three times three. He notices everything nice I do; our battles and arguments are few. I am so lovely he cannot ignore me; he is nevermore an absentee. We are together and in love. We are together and in love. We are together and in love.' Light the candle as you come to the end of your wording. Circle your hand above the flame in a clockwise or counter clockwise motion depending on your intent as you say three times "As this candle burns so does my magick work." Now raise your energy. Perhaps for a spell like one of the wording above self stimulation coupled with visualization would be in order. When you have sent your energy out ground and close the Circle (if used) as usual. Let the candle burn down to the pins and extinguish with a snuffer or hand clap. Wrap the candle in a dark cloth and keep it somewhere close by like under the bed. Carry the crystal with you. Now choose a second time about a week later as long as the moon phase is still agreeable and relight the candle on the altar. Repeat your wording and raise and send out more energy. Place the crystal so it is touching the candle and let the candle burn itself out completely. Carry the crystal or keep it on your altar until the spell has worked and then leave it in nature.

A Basic Written Spell

Items:

Pens with coloured ink appropriate for your intent or a quill and appropriate ink

Your own Book of Shadows

Two large candles in appropriate colours or white

A suitable incense

Form your intent and choose as auspicious moon phase; as well as perhaps moon sign and day of the week. Think about your putting your intent into words: How can it be said succinctly and perfectly clearly, yet powerfully? Prepare yourself ritually and cast a Circle if you can. Remember, a Circle helps your spell tremendously. Light the two candles and incense (if you have cast a Circle bring the incense to the altar from the Eastern Quarter). Open you book of shadows to a clean page and place it on the altar between the two candles. Spend a few moments focusing on your intent and then raise your energy. Now send out that energy seeing it pouring forth from you as a stream of light and direct some of it into the pages of your book of shadows and into your pen and ink. Sit comfortably with the book in your lap and write your intention. You could say something like "Lady of the Night and Lord of the Sun please hear me and make so my intent. It is that I get hired at blank. I work there happily and productively. My new salary covers all my bills and leaves me enough money to have some fun. I enjoy my job; it is exactly right for me and I do well there. The bosses' notice my excellent work and good opportunities come my way. Thank you" (If you are uncomfortable with involving the deities just write out your intent). Drip some wax from the two candles onto the page and hold the book in the incense smoke. Close it with a thump, extinguish the candles with a snuffer or handclap and ground and close the Circle if you have cast one. Try not to go back to that page or reread what you have written until long after your spell has worked.

There are so many spell types out there to try. Curses and Hexes, as I have already mentioned are not a great idea. A Glamour is a spell to change your appearance and using one is commonly called 'throwing a Glamour.' This might be as simple as wearing grey and standing in front of the mirror visualizing yourself hidden in a swirling mist for invisibility before you go out, or it might be as complex as a beauty spell that involves empowered facial products, a candle spell and new health regime. A jinx more commonly refers to an item that "has a jinx on it," as in it is believed to be unlucky or it causes problems for its possessor. It might also refer to something important to you, such as getting into a school or winning something and when someone talks about it, you say "Oh don't jinx it!" meaning 'let's not talk about it until it is secure.' Whatever the need or desire there will exist a spell to suit it, as all around the world, no matter the culture or colour or creed people have the same problems and wants. Sometimes you will find a spell so perfect you know it will work for exactly what you want. But whenever possible try to draft your own spells or put your own spin on them to suit your intent.

Virtually all spells that you do will have an intent that helps manifest what you desire, and that is one of the most important factors. For instance, I do a kind of spell at least one night a week that is based almost entirely on intent. As I lie in bed at night beside my better half I picture him completely surrounded and filled with a brilliant blue light of protection while I repeat the mantra "Happy, healthy, safe and well," in my head three times of seven repetitions each time. Does this spell need any specific correspondences or timing? No, but it is a spell of intent nonetheless. The one time a spell may not have a specific intent is if it's an unconscious spell. When you place a piece of jewellery or clothing on someone or cook them a meal that can turn into very powerful spell almost before you know it. Many things can, even strong thoughts as you do a repetitive action. This is not a bad or scary thing. Think of the act of putting an engagement ring on someone; this little act has the power to change lives in a very real and almost always positive way. As I said before, do not be afraid of magick. Just be self aware and in touch with the world around you, and use your magick wisely. A witch doesn't like to settle for last place or just 'good enough.' A witch's spells can change his or her world for their own good and the good of others and therein lies one of the glories of witchcraft.

11: A WITCH'S CIRCLE

What is a witch's or magick Circle? Also known as "Erecting the Sacred Temple," or "Building the House of Magick," the magick Circle is an old or even ancient concept, believed to come originally from ancient Babylonia. Almost all modern practitioners of Wicca and witchcraft have a concept of the Circle. Its uses are many: in Wicca it is the creation of a sacred space for ritual, and in many traditions it is used as protection, as well as a vessel to hold in energy until you are ready to send it on its way. It stands between worlds, not entirely of this world, yet not fully in the realm of spirits either. It is a tremendous aid to focus and concentration. It is a specialized magickal area for you to carry out your workings. Growing up at Killiecrankie I was fortunate enough to have a Circle always around me to focus magick and protect us, but we still cast them on the lawn often for spells, Sabbats and rituals, such as drawing the moon into ourselves.

In Wicca and some other paths the creation of a Circle involves making a consecrated or unprofane space for workings. Those with strong Celtic roots may believe that all natural space is already sacred and the Circle is more to make a barrier to hold and collect energy and power. In the past when the population was smaller and natural spaces were more prevalent than those with a human footprint no doubt there were more wild areas with the touch of Mother Nature and Jack of the Green upon them. In days gone by the Circle would have nearly always been cast outside, under the moon and far away from such modern contrivances as power lines, garbage trucks, or even other dwellings. In today's world we find that it may be quite difficult to find an outdoor space untouched by humankind. Sometimes we may have no choice but to erect our Circles indoors. So, while the Celtic notion that there is no need to make any part of Earth sacred for it is already is a lovely one, it can be hard to apply in this day in age. Therefore, unless you can find a totally wild spot for your Circle, some level of cleansing is a good idea.

Some folk suggest that a Circle should be cast for every spell, ritual and occasion. This would be great to be able to do, as Circles lend an energy of their own and help set the mind on the workings, but it is not always possible. In the case of Sabbat observance, for instance, I am not always able to celebrate outside or cast a Circle. A Circle will make your spells more powerful and effective, will make communication with the deities and ancestors easier and is a wonderful aid to divination and meditation, so when it is possible to cast one do so as it is a very useful tool. Circles can be cast indoors with a little adaptation, and if you live in a city this may be far preferable to using a park or other public space as privacy is important. The magick will not automatically be ruined if strangers stumble upon you, but your concentration may falter and any doubts that form have more negative effect than anything else.

The first thing you will want to do is become intimately acquainted with your chosen invocation or casting method. I provide one below but there are dozens available in books and on the Internet. You may wish to create one completely your own eventually, based on the deities you feel closest to or your heritage. The basic Circle consists of four quarters which are called and often represented with elements, and always candles. Some of us also bring the fifth element, spirit, to our Circle. The deities are invited to be present to witness and aid the work, depending on your belief. You will want to have an altar set up with your tools and any correspondences you may be using or any Sabbat items. Special words are said at each quarter and to create the Circle itself. You will want to read these over in advance many times, perhaps setting them to a tune or in a chant form. You do not absolutely need to memorize the whole casting and you can certainly bring the wording on a few sheets stapled together in order, but you don't want to have to refer to them too often. It interrupts the flow. Also it need not be word perfect, and may in fact be slightly different every time, as long as the spirit of it remains intact. Make sure to assemble everything you need in advance and take a quick ritual bath or wash up before hand. As detailed in *A Witch's Body of Ritual*, you should prepare yourself and your space. A Circle for one witch is usually nine feet in diameter; one for a coven may be larger, perhaps twenty seven feet. Many like to mark the boundaries of the Circle with salt and herbs, stones, or a specially measured rope. If you are outside the perimeter could be marked by drawing a line with a sword or knife point in the earth. (Do not use your athame for this.) You may choose to have no marking at all, as long as you can keep a clear idea of the edges in your head.

Another important point to remember is that while it is commonly referred to as a Circle, the magick space is really a sphere. You should concentrate on the fact that it is such and is not just flat on the ground. It should go over your head, all around you and even stretch slightly under the ground at your feet. We like to visualize it as a glowing blue ball of light, but you may wish to think of it as white, purple, silver, or another colour appropriate to the working. The four quarters are most commonly divided as follows, especially in Wicca:

North: Green, Earth, Gnomes, Bowl of Salt, winter, wisdom, and Crone.

East: Yellow, Air, Sylphs, Incense, spring, intellect, and Maiden.

South: Red, Fire, Salamanders, additional Candle, summer, action and passion, and Mother.

West: Blue, Water, Undines, Chalice, autumn, emotions, and also the Crone.

Centre: Purple, Spirit, pentagram, all, all are one.

There are many variances in these quarter breakdowns. For instance the use of Four Airts (Airt being a middle English word from the Scottish Gaelic meaning 'compass point,') holds that North is Air, East is Fire (due to sunrise), South is Earth and West remains Water. I have also heard of traditions where East is Fire, South is Air, West is Earth, and North is Water. The North/Earth variety is most common these days, but you may wish to adapt it based on the geography of your location, i.e. where the largest body of water lies and where the landmass is concentrated. One argument for using the order listed above is that it collects the male and female polarities as Air and Fire are masculine energies and Water and Earth are feminine. It is a good idea to align these energies by having two side by side for the sake of balance. Alternating the energies makes a balance as well though, so once again the choice is personal. The colours vary too; in the Four Airts method East is crimson like dawn, South white like midday light, West is the gray of twilight and North is the black of night. The choice is yours, but if you wish to use appropriate coloured candles at the four quarters you may find it easier to stick to the red/yellow/blue/green colour scheme. Sylphs, Salamanders, Undines and Gnomes are obviously creatures that are considered mythical and are said by those interested in the otherworldly to dwell in the spirit realm. They are not traditionally Celtic but are believed to have been brought in to Circle casting by the ancient Greeks, although Undine is said to come from the Latin word unda meaning 'waves.' Sylph is believed to come from the Greek silphe, meaning 'butterfly,' Gnome from the Greek gnoma meaning 'knowledge,' and Salamander the Greek salambe meaning 'fireplace.' There are, of course, salamanders in this world but they are quite a different sort. These four are said to be powerful creatures that lend their unique elemental energies to your quarters but are also said to be of prickly temperament. If you do choose to ask them to be present do so respectfully during your quarter calling by saying something like "Great watery Undines I humbly request you join me (us) here on this night and lend us your power," and so on with "Great fiery Salamanders, Great earthly Gnomes, and Great airy Sylphs."

Elemental representations are another choice you should make while getting organized for your Circle. I like to use them as I feel they lend more power and focus to the work. The small items used are a base form of sympathetic magick, such as a humble chalice full of spring water standing in for all the power of the seas, rain, rivers, clouds, waterfalls and so on, but I believe they help attune the mind. The same elemental representations that you have among your regular tools are perfect to place in their respective directions. In addition you will want to have four candles of the correct colours in the four directions, or simply four white or black candles, as well as fifth, purple or black or white in the centre with a pentagram or pentacle for Spirit. The altar, which may be a special portable table or simply a board, can be placed in the centre as well, although some prefer to set it up in the North or East. In my family we also like to have a balefire whenever possible at all Circles. These are traditional at most of the Sabbats and are usually lit outside the Circle, except at Ostara when it is lit inside the Circle in the Eastern quarter. A bank of candles of differing heights, maybe in the fire colours of red, orange and yellow or perhaps in colours geared to your intent can make a fine stand-in. This can be forgone if fire makes you nervous or you feel it will attract undue attention. Be sure to note any restrictions in your area about open fires and keep a large vessel of water or sand nearby.

When I was a teenager I had two girl friends who were interested in the Craft and we had the sun signs of Pisces, Aquarius, and Taurus, a water sign, an air sign and an earth sign. We were always on the lookout for someone of like mind who had a fire sun sign because we thought it would make an especially powerful Circle to have each person call their own element quarter. If you can ever arrange it, perhaps in a coven setting it might be interesting to try out, but it is important to note that one person alone can create a very effective Circle, as can a larger group, as long as they can work in accord and focus together.

To create your Circle, prepare as described in *A Witch's Body of Ritual*. Set up your altar, your correspondences, and your Sabbat celebration things, such as flowers, branches or loaves of bread. Place the four candles in their quarters, and the elemental representations, if you are using them. Do not light the quarter candles yet. Choose a type of incense in harmony with your working. Make sure to have something to eat and drink on hand for grounding or Earthing the Power. This might be traditional cakes and ale or wine, or it might be pure fruit juice and plain bread or crackers or fruit. Wear something special; this could be lovely robes of a natural material such as cotton or simply a certain outfit that you reserve for magickal working. Many of us like to work skyclad or naked, but this is not always possible or comfortable. Note that being naked in this case is less about sexuality and more about being totally free and removed from the mundane. Whatever you choose to wear make sure you are comfortable in it and unrestricted in your movements. Pantyhose and super tight jeans are not a great idea! The same goes for anyone else present. They should be comfortably dressed in special clothes, and they should sit and stand as you do. As you create the Circle they should stand inside its boundaries between the quarters, or near the altar, staying out of your way.

Begin by facing the altar and taking some slow deep breaths. If you feel it will help you to centre sit before the altar and meditate or simply breathe evenly with your eyes closed for a few moments. This casting assumes you are going to be using elemental representations. Light one or two solid bright candles on the altar in colours that suit or black and white. Have the lighter or matches in a pocket or in your off hand. Stand and take up your athame in your dominant hand. Raise it above you to the sky and say: "I begin now to build the House of Magick, may the Circle of Power grow up around me and draw in to me here and now!"

Walk clockwise to the Eastern quarter and say "I hail thee, Guardians of the East, powers of the dawn, air and the mind! I summon and stir thee to my Magick House!" Point the athame to the East visualizing a blast of yellow light pouring from its tip. Light the Eastern candle, and the incense. If there are others working with you they may clap briskly three times as you light the incense. Walk to the Southern quarter and say "I hail thee, Guardians of the South, powers of the day, fire and action! I summon and stir thee to my Magick House!" Point the athame to the south and envision a stream of red light pouring forth from it. Light the Southern candle, and a second candle that represents Fire. If others are present they can clap three times sharply as you light the second candle. Walk to the West and say "I hail thee, Guardians of the West, the powers of evening, water and the heart! I summon and stir thee to my Magick House!" Point the athame, sending a stream of blue light from it outward. Light the Western candle and tap the chalice three times with the blade of your athame. If others are present they can clap three times briskly in rhythm with your taps on the chalice. Walk to the North and say "I hail thee, Guardians of the North, the powers of night, earth and ancient wisdom! I summon and stir thee to my Magick House!" Direct the athame to the north and see a flow of green light coming from its tip. Light the Northern candle and tap the bowl of salt three times with your athame. Again, if others are working with you they may clap three times as you tap the bowl of salt. If you wish to work with the elementals, respectfully ask each one to be present after you light each quarter candle. Next, step to the centre of the Circle. Say "I hail the Power of Spirit, of all, and I summon, stir and beckon thee to my Magick House!" point the athame straight up to the sky and envision purple light emanating from it. Light the Spirit candle and touch the pentagram once with your athame. Any others present can clap once sharply as you tap the pentagram. Now, starting at the Northern quarter walk around the Circle's perimeter three times deosil (clockwise or sunwise), with your athame pointed toward the ground on the first round, outward at shoulder level the second time and above your head the third time shaping the Circle with a flow of coloured light from its tip. As you go chant "The Circle is formed, the magick's begun, I build the House, my (our) magick is done." Done in this sense meaning "carried out," rather than finished. Any others that are working with you may clap in a slow rhythm like a heart beat as you go. They should try always to clap in sync. Some like to carry bells in their off hand as they walk the Circle.

If you are requesting the presence of the deities stand before the altar and ask them now, respectfully in your own words. Sometimes a chant or song is used, or the ringing of bells. You could simply say something like "Lord and Lady, I (we) would like you to be with me (us) on this night, to witness and give power to my (our) work. Please join me (us) at my (our) Circle. Thank you." Continue standing before the altar breathing slowly with your eyes perhaps half closed, seeing and feeling the sphere of power pulsing all around you. It exists on a special plane, apart from the everyday world. Here you are protected from any outside influences, especially harmful malicious ones, be they of spirit or human origin. Here you can be free and safe. Here you build and raise as much energy as you can without it slipping away before you are ready. Proceed with your workings, raising energy for and carrying out spells as discussed in other chapters, drawing the moon into yourself (see *A Witch's Moon*) communing with those that have gone before, observing the Sabbats as detailed in *A Witch's Wheel of the Year*, or simply meditating or feeling close to the deities. Some Wiccans and other traditions state that you must always move deosil or clockwise within the Circle. This is a good rule to follow, as widdershins or anti-clockwise motions diminish rather than build, and what you will usually be doing is building or creating. The exception might be during a binding or banishing. Also, we close the Circle with widdershins motion.

After your serious work is complete many people like to dance, sing, drum or chant. The Circle is a highly charged atmosphere that usually lends itself to revels and joy, depending on the type of work you have been doing. You may in fact notice mental and physical changes within yourself as you cast and while you work inside it. It is normal to feel giddy or even "high" and have a sense of lightness. If you keep a small part of your mind on what is happening within your body during the building of the Magick House you may be surprised and delighted.

Like a house contains your belongings the Circle contains your energy safely until you direct it outwards. In a coven customarily the High Priestess will give a small signal when she feels the optimum amount of energy has been raised and should be released and then all the members concentrate on sending it out. If you are working alone or in a smaller group you will have to learn to get a sense of the right time. During sex magick this will be quite obvious, but when using other forms of energy raising this may take a little practise. When the energy is at its peak you can visualize it pouring forth through a point in the Circle, usually as a stream of appropriate coloured light.

If you need to leave the Circle before it is closed you will want to cut a doorway with your athame, (or wand, or pointer finger of your power hand.) It is important to see the opening, a clear spot like a glass door with light shimmering all around it. Step through and then draw the edges back together with the athame. Use the reverse actions to re-enter the Circle.

When everything is finished it is time to close the Circle. Starting in the centre you say "I thank thee Spirit for joining me on this night, and bid thee farewell." Extinguish the Spirit candle. Starting in the North and moving widdershins thank and bid farewell to all the Guardians: "I thank thee Guardians of the North/West/South/East for joining me on this night and bid thee farewell." Put out each candle with a snuffer or a sharp hand clap directly above it, or in this case blow it out, as you are blowing something away this time. Now starting in the North again and walking counter clockwise again walk three times around with your athame pointing to ground, shoulder height and sky, saying "Thrice round, magick sinks into the ground," several times on each pass around. Respectfully thank the deities for witnessing and perhaps boosting the power of your spell or ritual. If you have asked elementals to be there say a thank you and farewell to each at each quarter. Now sit at the altar where you will still have one or two candles burning, and eat and drink some of your cakes and ale or whatever you have. It may be necessary to imagine some blood leaving your head and going to your stomach to aid in the mundane function of digestion or to press your hands flat upon the ground and feel the leftover power flowing out of you into the earth. Everyone present should eat and drink something. When you feel yourself completely back to "normal" go ahead and tidy everything up, remembering to leave some of your grounding food out for the deities (often received by them through animals).

There are, as I said, dozens of different versions of Circle castings, or Invocations as they are sometimes called. Even the casting above is slightly different than the one I was first taught, although it is usually what we use now. Sometimes people refer to Invoking the Spirit, the elementals or even the deities. Generally, I prefer to think of it as asking them to be present. If you have a special connection to a totem animal or spirit guide it's a wonderful idea to ask them to be present at your Circle. Sometimes when people feel a strong bond with certain animals they like to call four of them in spirit form to be the Guardians of the quarters. Others erect Watchtowers mentally at each quarter to protect the Circle. Some like to finish with the phrase "The Circle is open, but never broken," which has a nice ring to it. Others may ask the Lord and Lady to help the magick to manifest before they bid them farewell. In some covens the members merely join hands and recite a short chant to create a magick Circle. A wand or sword may be used instead of an athame, or even a pointing finger. Only you will know which casting is right for you, and you may decide to adapt or rewrite one that you find for your own use. You will also want to make personal decisions on how formal it needs to be, whether to allow observers and whether they should be inside or out (I don't recommend having anyone present except someone you practise witchcraft with until you are completely comfortable with Circle casting), when you need to cast a Circle and when you can practise without one, and so on. Circles are usually cast at night. There is something very evocative about being in the dark, under the moon and stars, but they can certainly be cast in daylight or rain as well. If you wanted to specially honour the God you might cast a Circle under the sun as well. The main thing to remember is that a Circle makes a kind of transformation, both in your immediate physical surroundings and within yourself. The very creation of it is an act of magick and helps you to collect yourself, gather your thoughts, focus and power. The intense atmosphere within the Circle allows for heightened senses and awareness and makes energy raising easier. It will be simpler to focus and your focus will be sharper. If you are concerned with psychic attack or someone wishing you ill you will be free of it in the Circle and those that worry about harmful or mischievous spirits or ghosts can be assured they are protected from them within its confines. The Circle is one of a witch's best aids and you should try to become familiar and comfortable with casting and utilizing it to wield your magick most effectively. At the same time it can be a joyous and festive atmosphere, perfect for celebrating your life and chosen path.

12: A WITCH'S MOON

The moon is the brightest object in our sky other than the sun, and who among us hasn't spent time gazing up at her? To my family she has been an inspiration, a muse even, a guiding light to find our way home while out on the lake, and most of all, a source of magickal energy. She has been called many names over the centuries, Selene by the Greeks, and Luna by the Roman's, which is the root of such words as "lunatic" and "lunacy." Humankind has long observed the moon and used her cycles for our earliest calendars. An eagle bone tally stick recovered in France and dating back 13,000 years is believed to be one such lunar reference. Although the moon is an average distance of 384,400km from Earth she exerts enough gravitational pull to manipulate our ocean's tides and many believe she can affect our selves as well, considering our bodies are nearly 80% water. Some postulate that the full moon effect is caused by an increase in positive ions in the atmosphere, others by the fact that the added brightness causes people to be out later and get less sleep, and others say it is merely superstition. Many studies say that there is no such thing as full moon "madness" but I tend to think that the studies are simply not sophisticated enough to discover the truth or are not looking at the correct subjects.

When I was young my grandparents had an elderly woman friend who had worked in her youth at a mental health facility in Eastern Canada. This was some decades ago and conditions were primitive by today's standards, but she told stories of how the patients were dosed with cyanide on the days surrounding a full moon to keep them docile. This is disgusting, frightening and no doubt illegal, but it seems unlikely that the staff would have taken such drastic measures unless they had observed a keen need for them. All around the world emergency rooms, police forces, and ambulance workers prepare for each full moon by adding extra staff, and one study has shown that veterinarians should perhaps be prepared; incidences of pet injury do, in fact, increase during the full moon. People often make reference to the full moon's consequence's, there's a joke in our local pub about the "Full moon club, now in session" when people act up. It would be fair to say most people are aware of the moon's effects, whether they believe in them or not.

A witch, however, can make use of the moon in all of her aspects, not just when she is full. Different phases lend different energies to our workings, and in addition, we can utilize the energies of the zodiac signs that moon passes through every few days. The moon has four basic phases: New, waxing, full, and waning. Within these four aspects are sub categories: waxing crescent, when the moon is a small slice on her right side, waxing half, when she is half lit on the right, waxing gibbous, at three quarters and waning gibbous, three quarters again, the left side, waning half, when the left half is illuminated, and waning crescent when she appears as a small sliver in the shape of a C. A good way to tell by sight if she is growing or shrinking is to remember that the C shape indicates contracting or getting smaller. Through all her aspects she is available to lend her energies to our spells and magick, especially if you are working at night, which among my family has usually been considered preferable for many types of workings.

A new moon is a natural staring point. When the moon is dark it time for beginnings, gathering together resources for a project, planning how you will proceed, and creating. Magick now can be focused on starting fresh, making new beginnings and growing things. This is the seedling of your magick from which everything will come. During the waxing crescent, half, and gibbous stages of the moon you can focus on creating, building, making things larger and more powerful. This is a time for working magick that will increase things and strengthen them, such as wealth, health, love bonds, travel plans, beauty, protective shields and the like. Picture, if you can, the moon as large silver cauldron that is being stirred faster and faster in a deosil or clockwise motion. As she grows in size and visibility the liquid is spinning faster and faster toward a culmination. During the waxing moon you can cut or trim hair to have it grow back faster, as well as finger and toenails. You should prune plants now that you want to grow back stronger and more abundant. You can work on your health and vitality, concentrating on manifesting the things you would like to achieve more of, bigger muscles, more stamina, and more energy. For sex and love you would work on things you would like to have in your relationship, more, better and longer sexual encounters, more intimacy and togetherness in your partnership, or, if you are single and looking, more confidence when meeting people and more partners to choose from. For beauty and looks magick work on things that want generating, such as thicker, longer eyelashes, huge luminous eyes, and smoother skin, big welcoming smiles. This is a good time to make travel plans, collecting information, planning, adding to your itinerary.

The full moon is culmination. If you are performing a spell that takes several days to complete it is a great idea to have it finish on the night of the full moon. The full moon is a good time for fertility magick, as it has a ripeness and fullness that is sympathetic to a healthy, very pregnant woman. The full moon is the finish of growth, the height, the commencement. In our family we like to honour the full moon with an outdoor ritual whenever possible, which follows below. She is the Lady of the night, and appeals to the Goddess are made now. The full moon smiles on mothers, animals, women, maidens, and this is a good time to speak to her about spousal abuse, young children, pets or farm animals, and lost loves or those you love in secret, such as a young girl's crush. It's a beautiful time to be outside, bathed in her light and can lead to passionate sexual relations and much revelry. There were those among the old aunts in my family that cautioned strongly against letting young girls sleep with the light of the full moon bathing their beds, but this was in a time where sex before marriage was unheard of and there was still some fear of a young woman's natural sexuality. Use the full moon also to celebrate the fullness of your life and the achievements you are proud of and things you are pleased with.

The waning moon is for banishing, decreasing, and uncrossing. Picture again, the large, silvery cauldron of liquid being stirred; only this time it is being stirred widdershins or counter-clockwise. The motion is slowing, the tempo less and less furious and intense. During the waning crescent it all but ceases. This is the time to slow things, to be rid of things, to destroy things. This is not dark or scary though, this can be a wonderful opportunity. Think of things you may wish to rid of in your life, debt, wrinkles, extra pounds, negative thoughts or fears, weeds, bad habits, annoying relatives... (Okay, that one is pretty is difficult to be rid of!) But in all seriousness, this is an excellent time to deal with these things. Do rituals and spells to rid yourself of excess, of doubts, of things you no longer need. This is time for break ups, for removing someone or something from your life, for cleaning house, spiritually and physically. If you want to go longer between haircuts and trimming your nails attend to them now. If you are tired of pruning your hedges and cutting your lawn do it now and it will take longer before you need do it again. Get rid of garden pests now, start a diet, do a ritual or a treatment to be rid of pimples, wrinkles, body hair you do not want. In fact, do both, a treatment *and* a ritual, combining them for maximum effectiveness. If you destroy or remove something now, less will come back in its place. For money magick now focus not on increasing wealth but having less debts and financial obligations. For travelling, think of a trip with less or no problems or snags. For love magick, work on what you would like to decrease in your relationship; less conflict, less time spent apart. If you are looking for someone new focus on being less nervous, less shy, or whatever you worry about in yourself. This is time for decreasing and banishing negativity, be it self-created or from an external source. If you think that someone is wishing you ill or trying to hurt you now is time to banish or bind them. Got an ex who won't take the hint? Do a banishment during the waning crescent. Cut photos of the two of you together apart and get rid of items you owned or bought together or that remind you of them. Anything you that want to decrease should be taken care of now, and depending how strongly you want to decrease it do the working according to the amount of light left in the moon.

The moon's phases are a powerful aid to work with, but there are also moon signs to consider. Every 2 to 3 days the moon moves through a new zodiac sign. In addition to your sun sign, the zodiac sign that the moon was in during your birth has a strong effect on your personality. For example my husband I both have a Sagittarius moon which makes us love travel and adventure. It is said that having the same moon sign as your partner makes you very compatible and can overrule you sun sign compatibility. In terms of working with these energies and incorporating them into your spells and rituals a good almanac is useful, be it one for farmers or magickal people, and also, the information can be found for free online. The energies available are:

Moon in Aries: Powerful spell booster, but be wary of hot headedness or impulsive behaviour. Anything to do with sports, and increasing anything.

Moon in Taurus: Dependable energy. Good for love spells and for cementing partnerships. Spells for beauty, protection, anything to do with cars, the garden, and prosperity.

Moon in Gemini: Anything intellectual or related to intelligence. Making large purchases. Meeting new people and creating new bonds. Technology and weather.

Moon in Cancer: Anything related to hearth or home. Work on a straying spouse or one with a wandering eye. Family issues and fertility. Real estate issues, spells to find a new home.

Moon in Leo: Attraction and beauty. Confidence and spells to gain more of it. Wealth and prosperity magick, luck. Leadership, moving forward, change, protection.

Moon in Virgo: Stability and grounding. Also good for prosperity financial planning, growing your nest egg. Health and healing, repairing things that are broken or wrong.

Moon in Libra: Best for love and sex magick. Great for dates and nights out with a partner, communication, loving your family, resolving conflicts. Good also for beauty and court proceedings.

Moon in Scorpio: Good for sex magick and lust but not as good for love and commitments. Spirituality and invoking guidance from the dead or speaking to them. For banishing, for secret desires, dark, intense spells and protection.

Moon in Sagittarius: Excellent time to travel, make travel plans, or do spells involving travel. For adventures and spells to grow more brave and bold. For diplomacy, anything to do with horses or the legal system.

Moon in Capricorn: Can be used in magick relating to the home and matters of family as a second choice to Cancer. Good for money magick, dieting, cleaning. To sell or be rid of something.

Moon in Aquarius: For truth, for learning. Also good for travelling, for politics, for beauty. A fine choice for love magick, especially to draw a new love to you. Spirituality and large purchases.

Moon in Pisces: Dream magick. Anything to do with alcohol or drugs or police. Fall more deeply into something such as love. Spirituality and learning about yourself.

The moon phase and zodiac sign can be combined in your spells, such as performing a love spell during a waxing moon in Libra or a spell to decrease debt during a waning moon in Virgo.

The moon is on an elliptical orbit which means at times she actually does approach us more closely. Her closest approach is called Periselene or Pongee and this is a time when her energies are stronger for us to make use of, as opposed to Aposelene or Apogee when she is further away and not quite as powerful, although she is always an influence. You can check the moon's position online, in better almanacs, or by simply observing her. When she seems huge in the sky she is probably closer and it is an excellent time to harness her power.

There are various folk names for the different moons of the year, which fall roughly into the months of a calendar year:

January: Quiet, Wolf, Cooking, Winter.

February: Ice, Snow, Hunger, Trapper.

March: Storm, Fish, Sleepy, Winds, Maple Sugar, Worm.

April: Planter, Frogs, Wildcat, Growing, Pink.

May: Bright, Flower, Milk, Dragon, Hare.

June: Horses, Mead, Strawberry, Rose, Windy.

July: Claiming, Buck, Blood, Summer, Hay.

August: Dispute, Dog Days, Green Corn, Sturgeon, Fruit.

September: Singing, Harvest, Mulberry.

October: Harvest, Hunter, Blood, Kindly, Falling Leaves.

November: Dark, Bitter, White, Beaver, Snow.

December: Cold, Bitter.

Usually once a year a "Blue Moon" occurs which is a calendar month with two full moons in it. This is a time for a special Full Moon celebration with wine, games and laughter, outside if at all possible.

During a regular full moon I was taught to take myself and my tools outside if I could, to quiet place with as little unnatural light as possible. In the city this is pretty much impossible; I use the park, the balcony or even just a dark room. If I perform the Full Moon ritual indoors it is important to me to go outside afterward and gaze at the moon for a time. Special supplies for a full moon ritual include using white, blue, purple and silver candles in your Circle instead of the usual blue, red, green and yellow and "Moon blend," sage, lavender, or any incense that especially evokes the moon and the Goddess to you, as well as your regular ritual tools. If you cannot get four candles in these colours (silver is tricky to find) four white candles would work as well. A silver chalice and white robes are particularly appropriate now, if you have them. A Circle is cast, as discussed in *A Witch's Circle*. Facing the moon you raise your hands above your head to her. Chant softly: "Lady of the Night, Silver Lady of the Sky, I am calling out to you, hear my Cry," repeat until you are focused, usually about 15 times. Now speak to the Lady, the Goddess, in her ripe, silver aspect. Do you have any special requests for her, such as someone you want to notice you? Are you or your partner trying to become pregnant? Or are you just thankful for her beautiful bounty and your own? Use your own words. After you have finished chant: "Lady of the Night, Silver Lady of the Sky, I honour you, give my thanks, and until next we meet, bid you goodbye." Next, it is customary to whirl about the Circle, clockwise, with your arms upraised. Focus on feeling free, powerful, fulfilled. If you are with others you may wish to dance in clockwise circles with your hands clasped until you are quite dizzy. White wine or mead, if you can get it, may be drunk now. It is a time of revelry and thanks for what you are proud of and grateful for, especially your own achievements, be they magickal or every day. Fertility spells, spells against spousal abuse, spells for animals, spells of the Goddess' protection and spells to get someone to notice you may be enacted. The Great Rite would be appropriate now, especially if doing fertility magick, but is not strictly necessary. After making merry under the full moon's light make sure you ground yourself by eating some cakes and drinking some wine or juice and close the Circle carefully as much powerful energy can be raised by the light of the full moon.

In many traditions this is known as 'Drawing down the moon'. Ancient texts speak of witches pulling the moon down from the sky and making her lie upon the ground. This is certainly an interesting thought, but in my family tradition we concentrated on bringing the full moon into ourselves, feeling the power of the Goddess' light and using the full moon to celebrate. There are many great rituals for Drawing down the moon, and it is worth exploring, but many seem to be variations on the same theme, both honouring the Goddess' lunar aspect and working with the power of the full moon.

Another thing that you should consider when making use of the moon is whether she is 'Void of Course.' This is a sort of lunar "down time" when the moon has left one zodiac sign but has not yet arrived in the next. At this time she is simply not available to utilize. This is a short period that is never more than a day and can be as little as half an hour. A good almanac will show this information, usually as 'Moon v/c' for a certain time period. Be aware of time zones and Daylight Savings time when checking the almanac, or looking this up online.

My family lore holds that the moon is actually full for four days. This is not astrologically correct, but what is meant by it is that for two days before and a day after the moon is truly full she can exert a stronger pull than usual on us, and that can cause people to behave strangely. The flip side of this is that we can access full moon energy for a longer period, although it is better to do your full moon ritual on the night that she is actually full.

The moon can also be used for cleansing, both of tools and self. When you obtain new tools, stones, altar tiles, bottle, jars and so on it is a great idea to leave them, perhaps resting in a dish of salt, in the light of a waning moon for one or seven nights before you ritually cleanse them. This can diminish any built up negative energies they may have collected and pre clean them. Conversely, to empower an object or tool it may be left in the light of the waxing moon for one or seven nights, ideally up until the night of the full moon which will culminate the empowering. They can then be charged with your own personal power and magickal intent. If you suspect an object to be tainted or to have absorbed any negativity it is especially helpful to do this extra step. If you have been through any kind of crisis or argument or general bad time you can ask the moon to help restore you. Once again, to diminish anything, such as fear, use the light of a waning moon as near as possible to new, and for building something, such as self esteem or confidence use a waxing moon close to full. It is best to do this privately, and if all possible to do it wearing a robe that will be removed so you are sky clad (naked). Bring a white candle, a soothing type of incense or one that makes you feel powerful, depending on your intent. You may or may not cast a Circle, I usually do not, but if you wish to, bring your elemental representations. Bring also your athame and/or wand, and a small snack and drink, as natural as possible, such as a fruit or bit of bread and juice or wine.

Find a quiet place where you will not be disturbed, outdoors is best. This may be very difficult, I have to wait until I visit my sister in the country, but you could do a self cleaning ritual indoors, as long as you bathe yourself in moonlight afterward. Light the candle and the incense and sit cross legged with your athame or wand across your lap. Without rehashing the events that led you here, focus on the feelings that you want to be rid of and what you'd like to achieve. Maybe you are cleansing yourself of fear, jealousy, or anger. Maybe you are wishing to be braver, stronger, able to make the right choices. Take deep breaths, centring yourself and becoming calm and focussed. You may have strong reactions now even though it may have be awhile since the negative event, but that is perfectly fine. When you are ready extinguish the candle with a snuffer or handclap so you are bathed only in moonlight and remove your robe. Stand in the light of the moon and raise your arms to her. Speak to her, addressing her as Lady of the Night or Silver Lady. Using your own words explain what brought you here and what you'd like to feel and be. Clean, fresh and free or strong, brave and powerful. If you are removing the remains of a negative event feel the power of the moon's light stripping away all the hurt, worry and fear that you have carried. She can make you anew and clean away all the negativity within you. If you wish to embolden yourself feel her magick filling you with light and power, making you whole, strong and glorious. The moon's light is versatile and extremely potent. You may feel dizzy or 'buzzed` afterwards, so eat a small snack and have a small drink, pouring out the rest of your cup onto the ground. Thank the Lady of the Night. Point your wand or athame toward her, pouring your gratitude along its length. Salute her with your tool and bid her goodnight. As you dress and prepare to leave feel the new sense of wholeness and lightness the moon imparts. The magick of the moon is a great and largely untapped resource available to those who honour her. I like to salute her often, just with a nod or wave if I am with people, and feel the magickal sense both of comfort and strength she can lend to us all.

13: A WITCH'S SEX MAGICK

Sex and sex magick can certainly be touchy subjects (no pun intended), but they really shouldn't be. Before I go any further I'd like to categorically state that you should only try the things laid out in this chapter if you are comfortable with them and find they interest you. It is a totally personal choice, a *very* personal one, in fact, and being a witch doesn't ever mean you have to do things that you don't feel right about. That being said, there is nothing dirty, sinful, shameful or "wrong" about our normal drives and physical needs. The witches in my family have always found it very strange that such a big deal has been made over something as natural as sleeping or breathing, but the fact remains that most religions do attempt to wade into people's bedrooms and tell them what is "right" and "wrong." Admittedly, as religious doctrines start to lose their stranglehold on people and we embark on even more enlightened times this is less of a problem, but there are still many people who come from strict upbringings and have fear and guilt associations with sex. This is difficult for them to deal with and can even be dangerous as some studies have shown that young people who feel large amounts of guilt regarding sexual activity can fail to take precautions to protect themselves from sexually transmitted infections and unplanned pregnancies. They are so worried that what they are doing might be wrong they don't want to give it proper attention or may even want to block it out and this is very risky behaviour.

Why did religion get mixed up in our sex lives in the first place? Obviously there is some sort of connection as all major religions seem to have something to say on the matter, with the possible exception of Buddhism (Buddhism doesn't seem to concern itself too much with such mundane matters as sex, but does suggest that adherents refrain from "sexual misconduct." As intriguing as *that* sounds it is not immediately clear what exactly it might be). Not being an expert on all the various major dogmas (and not wanting to offend anyone), I can only say that the theory in my tradition is basically that the Christian Church has long had goals of control, and that maybe a group of self-righteous men, deciding that they knew what was best for the masses felt that making pre-marital sex a sin would cut down on unwed mothers and the spread of diseases. In times gone by, being a single mother was a very difficult life (it isn't exactly easy today either), and it does make sense that if you are going to raise a family you should be in a committed partnership if it is possible (then one partner can provide while the other cares for the children, as is seen in many partnerships in nature or both roles can be shared). But the view of sex as "sin" is really very outdated.

The fact that the last Pope said something along the lines that sexual relations within marriage are a way of imitating the Creator's generosity and fecundity suggests that even Catholics (masters when it comes to instilling guilt and shame) allow that sex within marriage is not wrong or dirty. So it's really sex outside of marriage that's supposedly so offensive, not sex itself. But in this day and age, when health is taught in many public school systems, with the advent of the Pill and the availability of inexpensive protections against unwanted pregnancies and disease one has to ask oneself is that attitude really relevant at all? It is, of course very important to be emotionally ready to get into a sexual relationship and this point varies hugely from person to person, but once you are there simply shouldn't be the type of qualms there used to be. It is one thing to decide to wait for the right person and it is lovely to be committed to one person, but if that is not a lifestyle that suits you is there any reasoned, intelligent argument for feeling badly about it? Sure, three hundred years ago if you wanted to be certain you weren't going to catch syphilis you would do well to marry a virgin, but things are so different now this is really an archaic way of thinking.

Most witches (and for the most part neopagans as well) take a very different view on sex. The famous *Charge of Goddess* written by Doreen Valiente and used by most Gardenarian adherents (and others) states that "All acts of love and pleasure are my rituals" (Doreen Valiente incidentally has many interesting things to say on the subject of sex magick in her books). This could be a general summation of the attitude toward sex most witches hold today. That the Goddess and God gave us eyes to see with, mouths to taste with, and bodies capable of such great pleasure in order to worship them in this way, rather than repress these desires. Repressing natural needs is even thought to be unhealthy and to possibly lead to psychological problems and obsessive behaviours. Why are we ready for love making in all seasons instead of just once or twice a year like many species if we are not meant to do it? How can denying one's very nature ever be positive?

With that in mind we broach the topic of sex magick, of which there are many varieties. Many traditional covens include the Great Rite in their third degree initiations and in certain celebrations. It's funny, but you don't hear as much about the Great Rite these days, or at least it is not mentioned in many of the popular new witchcraft books. Perhaps this stems from a desire to cast the Craft in a benevolent and unthreatening light.

"See, what we witches do isn't scary or weird! We aren't having any wild orgies or any sex at all at our rituals!" This makes sense as witches do have a tough time being accepted as "normal" sometimes, but it is a shame to abandon such a beautiful ritual in order to do so. The Great Rite is not a wild orgy by any means, most of the time it is practised as a purely symbolic act in which an athame is dunked into a chalice. In the case of an actual Great Rite, all coven members who might be present leave the room or area and return only when the act is complete, and it is only preformed by an established couple who fully consent (I'm sure I don't need to tell you that no self respecting witch would ever force anyone into some kind of sex act they weren't comfortable with, nor would a self respecting witch be bullied or pressured into anything they weren't happy about doing. It is simply, to use today's vernacular, not how we roll).

The Great Rite is a holy act that personifies the opposite energies that make up our universe, namely male and female. In some cases, through ritual phrases and actions the Goddess is invoked into the woman or High Priestess' body and the man or High Priest makes love with his Goddess. The traditional phraseology states that the woman becomes a living altar, the ancient altar of all things. Again, we run against contention from Christians here who find the idea of a human altar blasphemous at the very least. Instead of saying "ahem, we were here first," the answer to this could be that a woman's body is our initial altar of worship, in the form of our mothers and from time immemorial in the form of the Mother Goddess. Life springs from it, after all. Where would any of us be without a woman's body? How can it be disrespectful or wrong to honour such a thing?

The traditional Great Rite contains a fivefold kiss, in which the man or High Priest kisses the woman on both feet, both knees, her womb, both breasts and then on the lips. They embrace during the kiss on the lips. This is again, simply honouring and venerating the beauty and bounty a woman's body is and provides and really isn't strange at all when you think about it. The kisses start on the right foot and ascend, or else form an invoking pentagram by going right foot, lips, left foot, right breast, left breast and back to right foot, followed by a kiss to the womb. When we perform the Great Rite we are honouring our Goddess, our natures, the opposing energies that make up so much of this world and the riches of a woman's body. Conversely, the God could be invoked into a man or High Priest's body and be worshipped by a woman or High Priestess. We are certainly thankful for men, men's bodies and masculine energies as well.

Another form of sex magick is used for energy raising, as we briefly discussed in *A Witch's Body of Ritual*. Many budding witches and magicians start out spell casting and get discouraged if they don't see immediate, dramatic results. Sometimes this can be caused by a lack of focus or poor timing but often the cause is a lack of magickal energy. One of the best ways for us to create passion and energy is through sexual excitement and release. This is a resource everyone can tap into if they can find a way to lose their inhibitions. Many people find that auto erotic work or self stimulation is fine place to start. The idea is to form your intention or purpose (sometimes called a telos) beforehand and keep it in your mind as much as possible during the act, and then to concentrate (again, as much as possible, and this may require practice) on sending it out at the moment of release. The intention could be for any kind of spell work that you would usually do, protection, prosperity, spirituality and so forth. There are those that advocate a form of sexual energy raising that does not include a climax, the reasoning being that there is no danger of the energy raised being "lost." It is instead kept or held onto and later utilized during a more formal spell or ritual. This is a matter of personal choice, and you may have to experiment to see what works best for you, but I have always found sending energy out at this powerful time to be especially effective.

Working with a partner to raise and release energy for a spell can be really amazingly powerful as well. While it is possible to create energy and direct it to a goal while having sex with someone without them having any idea about what is going on, it is morally dubious. You could say what they don't know won't hurt them but really it is so much better to have both parties aware and in sync. This is also a case where a little knowledge can be worse than none at all; it is far better to explain fully what you are attempting to achieve and how. If you have a partner in the Craft so much the better, you should be able to explain the idea easily, but if that is not the case it may be very tricky. Use careful judgement before approaching a boyfriend or girlfriend (or spouse) and saying "Honey, I want to try some sex magick tonight." They might be delighted or completely freaked out, especially if they are sexually repressed in any way. You will know best whether it is a good idea to try and introduce this form of magickal working. If you are unsure of the response you will get you could start off by saying that there are witches who practise sex magick and see what type of reaction your partner has.

If you have a partner onboard (or when you are working by yourself) you may want to set a mood with white, red, or pink candles, or different colours based on your intent. Delicious smelling incenses and oils can be a treat (always skin test oils before applying them to sensitive areas) and any spell correspondences that are appropriate could be on hand, even close beside you or underneath you, depending on what they are. Sexual energy raising with a partner is not necessarily all about intercourse. Charged glances, flirting, caresses that make the hairs on the back of your neck stand up, and all forms of sexualized touching and play are ways of raising power and energy. Generally the most potent way of sending this energy out is to do it at culmination, but how you get there is up to you and your partner. Simultaneous climaxes are highly desirable for spell work but are not always possible, so just try to have both parties focus on the intent at the time even if only one of you has got there.

Some people like to use the combined sexual fluids to anoint a talisman or charm that is related to the spell. Some people find this repulsive. As always, personal choice is involved. Sometimes words or phrases related to the spell are called out at the crucial moment such as "Prosperity in the new business!" Sometimes it is utterly impossible to remember some statement you are supposed to be making and you may want to practise a bit.

Taking an herb infused bath before hand or enjoying a lover's meal of favourite foods can help to focus and relax. You want to be happy and calm with feelings of perfect love and perfect trust to achieve optimum results. It might be best not to attempt sex magick with someone who you barely know or who you still suck your stomach in around. You want to be attuned to each other and able to get into a rhythm. During the act itself try give attention to building and strengthening the energy, almost feeling it as visceral thing between you. Some traditions refer to "magickal children," or spirits that are created through lovemaking and sent out to do your magickal workings. If this idea works for you go for it. There is a school of thought that suggests the man should hold off on climaxing as long as possible but that is not a must. It can sometimes raise more energy as more time is spent and it sometimes optimizes a woman's chance of getting there too, but each couple will be different. Same sex couples can have great results with sexual energy rising too, of course. The same principles apply. Anyone may find it hard to keep the intent on their mind and some suggest "backgrounding," it until the last minute, but it is usually better to try to keep it in mind all along. Practise makes perfect! In terms of sexual energy raising for healing.... well that's a tricky one. What if you know the person you are doing the healing for would be totally disgusted by the thought of what you were doing to help them? It's probably better not to do it then, but each situation is unique. Use your best judgement. If you yourself are thinking it's a little weird then it's probably not the best method to use, but remember it is natural, normal, delightful, and one of the most effectual ways to raise tension and therefore energy for spell work.

In the last decade or so there has been a lot of buzz about Tantra or Tantric Yoga, related to Vamachara. Quite a few celebrities are practising it and it seems to be an interesting and rewarding path. Traditional practitioners point out that sexuality is just one aspect of a very involved study, but it is worth mentioning that ritual intercourse is used to help enter the "structure of the universe." There are a variety of methods used to prolong sexual excitement and lovemaking sessions, and some practitioners learn to achieve multiple and long lasting climaxes. Sometimes Tantric monks make love with females who represent the Goddess, putting one in mind of the Great Rite, and Tantric Yoga is no doubt worth exploring if it interests you.

Yet another form of sex magick is used to strengthen the bond in a couple. You are exchanging energy every time you make love, even exchanging part of yourself. The very act of sex in general can strengthen a couple, bringing them closer and making them indivisible in a very basic way. I think we all have some expectation or hope that sex should be or has the potential to be "magickal" with the right person, but how many of us actively try to make magick when we are having sex? This is definitely something that bears thinking about and investigating. Again, correspondences for love could be on hand and perhaps even involved. Use your imagination. Hot wax is an interesting substance, as are feathers, different fabrics, silk ribbons and so on. There is a sort of joke that people use to describe something really wonderful as a "religious experience," but why not make it be one for real? You could try to plan out a time for this, but it is probably better to plan what things you'd like to try the next time it comes up naturally. Telling your partner that you want this lovemaking to bring you closer and to be really special, setting the scene with candles and other correspondences, visualizing, and focusing during the time on how each beat of your hearts makes you one or tightens a knot that holds you together, etc. are all good things to try. Fluids collected, perhaps with a tissue and saved from a magickal love making session can be very powerful in love charm bags to keep your bond strong, if you don't find the idea repellent. This type of magick can have an amazing effect on a couple, especially if you know it can really work.

Some techniques for letting go of guilt and inhibition include becoming more comfortable with your own body and your partners as well. As mentioned above a soothing bath can be very nice, and if your tub or shower is big enough it can be great for two as well as one. Deep breathing and letting the mind go blank in a sort of meditation can help you to relax and be more at one with yourself and your surroundings. Some people like to explore their own bodies with a mirror. Some couples like to get involved in dance classes or giving each other massages. A bit of light exercise can go far to boosting your self-confidence, as can pampering yourself with lovely lotions, shampoos, and a manicure or pedicure. Spend some time in dim lighting, simply running your hands over your skin and cataloguing the things you like about yourself. The human body is a miracle and is never truly ugly. A healthy sexual appetite is good for you. Sexual activity releases tension and stress and helps a couple become closer and live a happier life together. It should be fun and you and your partner should be able to laugh and joke and be equal participants in all the pleasure available to you. Sex is beautiful!

Different types of magick can be made during auto erotic practise as well. By focusing hard on someone during a session and using visualization you can often make them notice you the next time you see them but this is an ethical grey area. Consider whether you would want someone to do this to you before you decide how to proceed. You can work on goals for yourself like being happier, more confident and therefore more attractive with self stimulation. Sometimes auto erotic "work" is ideal for this type of magick because you have more control over its duration and how much energy you can raise to direct toward your intent. This is a good time to turn your focus inward and help improve your own attitudes, whether about your self-image or your feelings about sexuality.

Correspondences for general sex magick or sex magick to become closer as a couple are mostly the same as love correspondences, as discussed in 'A Witch`s Correspondences.' In addition, the colours red and maroon, cloves, red stones, hibiscus, ginger, ginseng, lavender, quartz, thyme, oysters, asparagus, cardamom, gardenia, your own spirit or totem animals, and your own bodily materials such as perspiration and hair can be especially powerful and helpful.

There are, of course, other types of ritualized and magickal sex. It is probably one of the oldest forms of magickal power creation. Many people feel things during sex that they never feel at any other time, and some of those things can be harnessed to help do your will. For some it is as close to a mystical, transcendental, or "otherworldly" feeling as they ever come. Sex is an almost super magickal resource that it would be a shame to overlook. As with all things try to go forward with an open mind and you may surprise yourself with what you can achieve.

14: A WITCH DIVINES

The word "divination" comes from the Latin "divinare" which can be translated to mean "to foresee" or "to be inspired by God." The desire to look into the future and answer burning questions is certainly as old as humanity itself and various methods of divination can be traced back hundreds and or even thousands of years. Divination can be a witch's ally for many reasons, not the least of which is our desire to take action in life rather than letting it pass by us, out of our control. There are many, many methods of divination, some of which have gone out of fashion over the centuries, such as the ancient Greek Oracles propensity for killing sheep and goats and examining their livers for insight into coming battles. Some other now less popular methods of divining the future include Alectryomancy (by cocks eating grain), Icthyomancy (by fish), Gyromancy (by whirling in circles), Belomancy (by arrows), and Cattabomancy (by brass vessels).

Today, a witch is more likely to make use of a crystal ball or other scrying vessel, a tarot deck, pendulum, loose tea leaves, the stars, runes, or perhaps the ancient *Chinese Book of Changes,* otherwise known as the *I Ching.* There are four main types of divination: omens, such as seeing a black cat (lucky in my family tradition); augury, which governs dowsing as well as reading the future through groups of animals; spontaneous, which deals with bibliomancy (putting a finger on a random passage in a book) as well as reading auras; and sortilege, which is the interpreting the casting of lots, be they cards, stones, runes and so on. Here, we deal primarily with sortilege, as well as the use of a pendulum. It's worth noting that there have been many cannons, edicts and public regulations over the years regarding divination. For a long time predicting the future was forbidden in many parts of the world and capital punishment for doing so was at times the legal norm. However, in this enlightened day and age anyone in the Western world may practise divination, whether they are a witch or not and there are many fraudulent practitioners out there. It is not really ethical to accept money for readings although one may do so if they are in real need. Bartering for services or favours makes a nice a solution, and free readings for friends and family are usually met with delight, if you have the time and inclination.

The *I Ching* or *Book of Changes* or *Classic of Changes* dates back to long before Christ, by either hundreds or thousands of years, depending on who you ask. Originally, yarrow stalks were used, but that practise died out and today coins are commonly utilized. Shiny and tarnished coins may be used or else the head and tails sides of the coin. This determines whether each cast of the coins is yin or yang, i.e. shiny or heads for yang, and tarnished or tails for yin. In the *I Ching* you toss three coins from a place of concealment, such as a cup, six times to form one of 64 hexagrams, all of which have meanings based on the patterns of yin yang (or positive and negative). You may want to record the sequence of each toss of the coins. Each hexagram has a predetermined significance which can be found in many great books on the subject or for free online. The main thing to remember about the *I Ching* is that it does not answer yes and no questions directly but shows you patterns and information that can help you in your choices. The *I Ching* has two functions, in addition to divination it is a compendium of cosmic principles and is very interesting in its own right. Although it is said to be the stuff of the poorer classes, pavilion soothsayers and small town oracles, this lends it a certain authenticity.

Scrying, also called peeping, seeing, or crystal gazing, comes from the English word "descry" which means "to make out dimly," or "to reveal." It may be done in a crystal ball, a dark bowl of water or dark mirror, a bowl of coloured ink, in the coals of a fire or in smoke, fog, or mist. The ancient Greeks used a dark vessel of oil, the ancient Egyptians used ink, blood, and other dark liquids, and the ancient Romans used shiny objects and stones. A text called the *Shahnameh* dating from pre-Islamic Persia (Iran) gives an account of wizards using the cup of Jamshid to observe the seven layers of the universe. Any reflective or translucent surface may be used but most witches favour a traditional crystal ball, darkened mirror, or else a black bowl filled with water. If a glass or lead crystal ball is used it may be of any size, the bigger ones are popular perhaps due to the iconic image of a gypsy or wise woman reading fortunes in a large ball the size of a grapefruit or bigger. I use one about the size of a lime and do fine with it; the larger ones can be prohibitively expensive even if they are only glass. It should be free of bubbles and polished regularly to remove fingerprints. They come in a large variety of colours nowadays, and that is perfectly fine, you may wish to choose a colour based on what the majority of your work will be about, such as red for love divining. I personally prefer a clear ball, but it is a matter of taste.

If a stone gazing orb is to be used, clear quartz is traditional, but they also come in amethyst, beryl, agate, obsidian, calcite and others. Any of these make fine divining balls, although some may find that the flaws they contain can be distracting. As with all Craft items, try to handle gazing balls before purchase and see how you feel about them. Any type of crystal ball or gazing orb should have a stand or small pillow or even just a special cloth that it rests on while you work with it. They should be stored in a dark place; some say wrapped in black velvet, but any soft cloth should be fine.

Mirrors made of obsidian are also traditional, but a concave piece of glass painted on the bottom (the outside) with matte black paint will work nicely, as will commercially available dark mirrors, although it is, as always, better to handle them yourself rather than obtain one through mail order. You could even scry in a pond or other still body of water. Some aboriginal American tribes scry in the steam they create in sweat lodges, and in the chapter *A Witch's Wheel of the Year* it is noted that scrying in the Samhain balefire is also traditional. Whatever method of scrying you choose it is most important to do it in a darkened room or at night, or on a dark cloudy day. Some folk like to have only a single candle for illumination, often with the flame reflected in the scrying vehicle. Images revealed through scrying vessels often appear right in your mind's eye or in the vessel as archetypes which may take some practise to interpret. In the beginning of each scrying session place your hands on the tool and think about the intent of the session and the questions you would like to answer. Remove your hands and try to relax and unfocus your eyes as well as your mind. With any divination, a trance like state is desirable.

The word tarot is said by some to come from the ancient Egyptian words for "royal road" although most agree that "picture cards," did not really come into fashion in Western Europe until the eighteenth century. Most tarot decks are organized into major and minor arcana. The major arcana include such cards as the magician, the empress, the sun, the moon, and justice. The minor arcana are comparable to regular playing cards, being the ace through ten of each suit. There are a huge variety of tarot decks available today, the *Vampire Tarot*, the *Goddess Tarot*, the *Fey Tarot*, the *Thoth Tarot*, the *Animal Tarot*, the *Pirate Tarot* to name just a few. You may find that one of the many out there appeals greatly to you or is designed by your favourite magickal author and resonates with you personally. That is great! Whatever you feel most comfortable with is probably the best thing you can use. I have always had the best luck with the *Rider Waite* deck, and this one is easily relatable to the majority of literature on the subject, but most good decks will come with an instruction book. Do take a look at the magician, the number one card in the *Rider Waite* deck and note how he has several of our magickal tools arrayed on the table in front of him. This deck makes use of cups or chalices, staffs or wands, pentacles or pentagrams and swords, which can stand in for athames. This is no doubt partly why I have always found it to be a good deck for me. Some people like to combine two decks of ordinary playing cards and use these for divination. This is interesting and works if you are in some kind of divining pinch, but can get confusing and may require a written key, as there are 78 cards in most tarot decks and of course only 52 in a regular deck. If you should care to attempt this you can use clubs as wands, diamonds as pentacles, spades as swords, and hearts as cups. For the major arcana you will need to assign cards from a second deck with a different backing so you can keep them straight, such as using a second queen of hearts for the empress and so on. In playing cards the nine of hearts is said to be the love card while the three of spades is ill omened.

Whatever deck you end up with, it is most important to handle them often, and become intimately familiar with the imagery of each. You will want to learn the given "meaning" of each card by heart, especially if you are going to give readings for others, but it is also important, perhaps even more important, to develop your own meanings for each card. What do you think of the pictures and what do they represent in your mind? What about the numbers? What suit do you like best and why? Which one do you like the least? Do any of the cards remind you of a specific person? Are any of cards "theirs"? You may wish to record this information in a divination journal or in your Book of Shadows. Personal feelings about each card can even override printed material on the subject. For instance, there are a lot of negative things written about the card the moon in the *Rider Waite* deck, but I have good feelings about the card and use it to represent myself in certain spreads. Having your own meanings for all the cards in your chosen deck will greatly enhance your readings and allow you to inject your own personality into the interpretations, which, let's face it, is far better than reading out the meanings from a script.

For all the different decks of tarot cards there are available there are probably an equal amount of spreads or arrangements of cards for fortune telling. The very most basic of these is to ask a question and cut the deck with your left hand, interpreting the card you turn up as a guide to your answer. Another very basic one is a three card draw, past, present, future. There is a simple spread regarding money that goes one card, another directly above it, the next to the right, and then two more to the right of that, top and bottom. These five cards, in the order they are drawn represent your financial situation in the past, now, in the immediate future, the fourth card means known factors affecting finances and the fifth, unknown factors affecting finances. My mother favours a version of the Celtic cross spread of ten cards.

The first is chosen to represent you or the person you are reading for. It is placed directly in front of you. Next, the top card of a shuffled deck is placed across it. This is what crosses or covers you, something that potentially keep you down. Now, a card is placed to the left of the first two. This is the recent past. A card to the right of the first two is the near future. A card above the first two is the best possible outcome for the situation. A card below the first two is what you have influence over. Next, four cards are drawn and placed bottom to top to the right of the future card. These represent, in ascending order, factors affecting the outcome of the situation, your home and/or heart, your hopes and fears, and the final outcome of the situation (or, if not yours, then those of the person you are reading for). Many alternate spreads are available in books and online free of charge. Become familiar with up to about half a dozen and use them as you see fit.

Shuffle the cards several times before each reading and either cut them three times with your left hand, or have the person you are reading for do it, also with their left hand. If you (or they) are left-handed, the right hand is used. When you are not working with your cards, store them in a dark place, perhaps in a cloth bag.

Tea leaf reading, also known as tasseography or tasseomancy is another iconic Gypsy image that is not as popular as it once was. My great aunt Nan was very adept at it and could be persuaded to give readings for all the young folk on the veranda at Killiecrankie. I only wish someone had written down more of her interpretations! There are however, several websites that give information on what all the images mean, and again, you will want to try developing your own set of meanings for each image. You will want to use loose tea leaves instead of tea bags, of course, and perhaps make use of one of the many speciality blends available. The use of coffee grounds for divination is thought to have developed in Italy and is also interesting to explore. Bubbles in your tea or coffee represent money. Lots of rising bubbles mean lots of money, while a few bubbles that appear to sink mean hard times. Strong tea can indicate a new friendship, while weak tea may indicate the end of one. Drink all but a tiny bit of the liquid and then turn the cup over onto the saucer, rapping it three times. The leaves will form into shapes that are then read. A cup of tea usually represents about a month's fortune. Time frames are estimated by the proximity of images to the rim of the saucer; things that will happen soonest are closest to the middle. If an image appears and then disappears it means the issue is becoming important now. Birds are said to mean bad luck, yet a flock of birds flying is good luck. A baby means small worries, and a house security. A chain represents a wedding or other partnership. Clouds can be troubles and coins mean money. Grapes mean happiness and abundance while a dog represents a friend unless you or the person you are reading for really doesn't like dogs, in which case it can mean an enemy. A fish is said to be good fortune while a leaf means a new life or a baby on the way. A cat in repose is a very good sign, but a stalking cat can mean someone causing discord in your life. A boat can be a journey or unsettled times ahead, while a horse means a journey that is sure to be pleasant. There are some very neat special cups and saucers for sale with different meanings on the saucers such as 'money' or 'love' (which are read based on the images that land on or near the words. For example, if grapes form near the word 'love,' you will be happy in love). These are great to buy if you get really into tea leaf reading. Try searching "tea leaf reading" on the Internet for lots of meanings, and do try to create your own meanings for images you see as these will be the most powerful and correct interpretations.

Pendulum divination, also known as radiesthesia, has been in use for many centuries, some say it can be traced back over 5000 years to the ancient orient. Nostradamus may have used a method of divination that involves a cup as well as pendulum. The stone, root, ring or other token was attached to a chain as we commonly do it now, but it was then hung inside a cup and the answers came in the form of taps. One tap indicated a yes, two a no, and more taps that the "spirit" answering the questions didn't know the answer. Ancient Romans used a tripod, a bowl made of metal alloy, and a ring attached to a wand. Today it is more common to have a pointer attached to a short length of chain, sometimes with a handle to help prevent incidental movement from your arm influencing the motion. It's also a good idea to have a small stone, ball, or token at the other end of the chain to keep it from slipping through your fingers. There are lots of readymade pendulums for sale in New Age shops and over the web, many types of stone are used, and copper is also a popular choice. Silver is good too, if you can find it. My regular pendulum is green moss agate which is generally lucky and relatively inexpensive, but quartz is a good choice, as is onyx, obsidian, or any stone that appeals to you. You may want to tailor your choice based on the intent of your work, like using rose quartz for love divination. In lieu of buying a pendulum you may want to simply use a ring on an ordinary necklace chain and this will certainly serve.

For your answers you can start off by simply using a piece of paper on which you have indicated YES on a horizontal axis and NO on a vertical axis. Later, you may wish to add other answers such as MAYBE and UNLIKELY which is fine to do as long the lines they are on are clear and different, perhaps radiating out from the origin like the spokes of a wheel. Some people like to use a talking board or Ouija board to spell out pendulum answers, and as you get more and more adept you might try maps for finding lost articles, or calendars for finding out exact dates.

Hold the pendulum about one inch above your paper or board. Relax and try and think of nothing but the question you have in mind. You might find it helpful to steady your elbow on a table, or stack of books, as your arm may get shaky after awhile and give you false indications. Some people like to use a pendulum in healings to help locate the source of an illness. In this case a person lies down and the pendulum is held over different parts of the body. Positive statements are made, such as "the problem is in the stomach." When the statement is correct the pendulum will start moving in a different way.

Ouija boards, which literally mean Yes-Yes boards, using the French and German words for yes are fun for parties and gatherings. Versions of these were used by the ancient Greeks and there are some lovely, elaborate types available today. You need at least one other person to use one though, and it is useful to have a third person present to write down any letters or words that are spelled out. Sometimes words are spelled out backwards or in other languages. If you think the person(s) you are using it with may be having a bit of fun with you, watch for stiff, jerky motion rather than smooth flowing results. Aliester Crowley was a fan of talking boards, and they can be very entertaining, but for serious divination work I suggest a method that you alone have control over the proceedings.

Perhaps the most common form of divination appears in most daily papers and that is divination by celestial bodies, or astrology. This is a subject on which there are countless fine resources available. It is worth remembering that divining by the stars and planets may be as simple or as complex as you would have it be. For example, most daily horoscopes are based on your sun sign only, that is the sign the sun was in during the day of your birth, but natal astrology goes much deeper than that and involves the position of the moon and other planets at the time of your birth as well the houses, your rising sign or ascendant sign and much more. Predicting your future or even the kind of day you will have then becomes more complex and tricky but it can be done with diligent study. A qualified astrologer can cast a natal chart for you and perhaps one for your partner with predictions for your life or your lives together. This is a good place to start learning about astrology, as understanding the why of predictions made about you can get you really interested in learning more.

Dowsing refers in my family to the use of a Y-shaped stick or special rods, often made of copper, to find water, minerals, or even gold or other precious metals. The rods or the two top branches of the Y are clasped loosely in the hands and the mind is cleared. It is important to quiet your thoughts except those related to what you wish to find. The rods or stick will then guide you in the correct direction. If you find you have an aptitude for dowsing and a desire to learn more there are dowsing societies in many major cities that you can join.

There are many fine sets of runes for divination on the market today. These are usually based on the Elder or Norse runes and will come with an instructional booklet. You could undertake to make your own set, using one branch (for uniformity) cut into slices about a quarter of an inch thick. Then a wood burning tool is used to inscribe one of the runes onto each slice. There are some very handsome stone rune sets out there, to make your own one of these would be more difficult but certainly rewarding. Of course, there is nothing wrong with using a set that you buy. Keep them in a pouch. For a reading, lay all of them out in front of you face up and pass you hands over them in slow clockwise circles. When your hands feel warm or tingly pick up the rune below them and add it to a line up. The order in which you are drawn to them as well as the meaning of each rune will help you with your predictions. You can also use the same spreads that you would use in tarot for rune readings. As with the tarot, handle your rune stones often and read up on the meanings of each, as well as working on developing your own feelings about what each one represents to you.

There are, of course, many other methods of divination that are in use today, as well as those which are not as popular now but that may appeal to you personally. When you are learning to divine you may want to try your hand at several methods, even a dozen before deciding on one or two or even more that you will pursue. It may take years to become adept at your chosen method(s) but try not to get discouraged. It is very rewarding to utilize divination in helping you to make choices and see what's coming. Start out by keeping your sessions short, no more than fifteen or twenty minutes at first, and recording immediately afterward anything you saw or felt or any questions that were answered. As with all Craft tools, cleanse and dedicate your divination items before use, as discussed in *A Witch's Tools*. It's a good idea to cleanse and purify yourself before you do a divination session, either with a ritual bath or by washing your hands and face, anointing yourself with essential oil (a dab of a type that you have pre-tested for skin sensitivity on the forehead, throat, chest, pubic bone, and the tops of hands and feet) and wafting incense smoke all around the room before beginning.

Correspondences for divination include white and purple candles (although any colour may be used and can be tailored to your intent) and white, black, purple or blue altar cloths or cloths spread out before you. Thyme, sweet grass, mugwort, marjoram, cherry, peonies, pennyroyal, meadowsweet, hibiscus, figs, cloves, and gardenia are all helpful to have at divining sessions, you may want to burn a dried and crushed handful of one or more of these, perhaps in your cauldron, before beginning. (Be aware of sensitive smoke detectors when doing this and keep a container of water about for safety). In terms of stones, hematite, crystal quartz, aquamarine, azurite, mica, moss agate, obsidian, onyx, lapis and possibly rainbow moonstone are useful to have on hand during divination. Sandalwood, frankincense, and lavender incense are good choices, as is any incense that you feel will be helpful. Lavender essential oil could be used, as well as rose and prepared vision or divination oils that often contain sandalwood. You can perform divination on any day, but Sundays and Wednesdays are especially good. A Gemini or Pisces moon is a good time for divination, but any moon sign will work. Of course you can perform divination on your altar, but it can also be done on a table or counter and you may not want to use your altar if you are reading for someone else as some people like to keep their altars private. The choice is a personal one.

In addition to purifying yourself and your space and perhaps having some correspondences on hand you will want to relax and unwind. You want your mind to be blank of anything except the questions you want answered. Take deep breaths and centre yourself for as long a time as you need before stating your intent. This might be something like "To find out what kind of new job Frank should be looking for," or "What can I do to get Sally to notice me?" or "What do the next six months hold for Jim that we do not know about?" Place both hands on the tool and think of your intent or state it aloud. It may help you to visualize your intent or questions pouring from your mind through your hands and into the tool, perhaps in the form of white or silvery light. When you are satisfied that your intent is clear lift your hands and begin. Continue to keep your breathing slow and regular and try to be very calm, relaxed and focused only on what you wish to reveal. If the answers you are getting are unclear try rephrasing the question(s). You may ask several questions at once but try to keep them to a general theme. Peace, quiet, dim light, incense smoke and emptying your mind except for the questions you are asking may induce a trance like state after a time and this is highly desirable. A trance state allows your mind to open and reveal things you may not be consciously aware of.

It may be asked why divination has been banned over the years, feared and considered evil. There is no easy answer but it may have been to do with the fact that it was (and sometimes still is) believed that the answers coming through the divination medium come from evil spirits or even the "devil." This is not true however. While it is possible that the helpful spirits of the deceased may occasionally lend an influence to divination, the answers you get almost always come from within. When you enter into a trance state you are opening the door to your subconscious and allowing parts of your brain to work that are usually inactive. You may, however, wish to respectfully ask the Goddess and God to bless your workings and help guide your tools.

15: A WITCH'S ADAGES AND ADVICE

This chapter is a bit of a miscellany of lore gleaned from the "old aunts," my mother and grandfather, and general knowledge that can be helpful in your everyday life as well as your magickal one. Some of these are just for fun and interest but I have found most of them to useful at different times in my life. Some people have pointed out that some of the tips in this chapter remind them a little of 'Good Housekeeping,' or other publications on domestic knowledge. Certainly this may be true, although some of the suggestions are of a more esoteric nature. The wise women in my family ruled and ran the household first and foremost. They may have had hired help, they may have been artists, wives, mothers and matriarchs as well as witches, but they were also keepers of the house. Witchcraft and household know-how are inextricably intertwined in my mind, and terms such as 'kitchen witch,' 'cottage witch,' and 'hearth witchcraft,' are common nowadays. Knowing practical solutions for everyday problems, having knowledge about plants and animals, being able to take charge of situations and handle them without losing your cool and using natural materials as much as possible are all parts of witchcraft as well as the domestic arts, and to me the two often go hand in hand. In short, these are simply things to bear in mind.

A black cat coming to you is good luck, as is a black dog. Encourage them to stay, if you can have a pet, and good fortune will follow.

Any cat that casually visits is lucky, and is thought to possibly be acting as or for a relative or loved one who has passed on and wishes to visit you and/or let you know they are alright.

An egg makes a fine substitute any time a living sacrifice is called for in any old, obscure spells you may encounter. Milk can also work for this in a pinch.

You can use the plant mullein (dried) as a substitute for an equal amount of graveyard dirt, should you come across a spell that calls for it and not wish to venture into a graveyard and dig up dirt there.

If you see birds in the field, usually magpies, their numbers have meaning: One for sorrow, two for joy, three for a girl and four for a boy, five for silver, six for gold, and seven for secrets not to be told.

Any unintentional mention (be it written, spoken, seen) of silver and gold in the same sentence is lucky.

The number 13, far from being unlucky is thought to be Brid's special number and thus lucky and a good omen.

Wishing upon the first star you see after twilight is especially lucky, but try not to tell anyone what you wished for. The traditional saying that goes with the wish is "Starlight, star bright, first star I see tonight, I wish I may, I wish I might have this wish I wish tonight."

If you spill salt do toss a pinch over your left shoulder, but this is more to do with avoiding waste in the future and not to do with "blinding the devil."

Knocking on (real) wood frightens away mischievous spirits who might hear what you are afraid of and try to make it come true as they often misbehave out of sheer boredom.

An east wind, in my part of the world, can bring a very fierce storm, or bad news.

Waste not, want not.

Haste makes waste.

A ring around the sun or a "sun dog" is a good omen.

If a bird defecates on you from the sky above it is said to be lucky but I have my doubts about this one. I tend to think it is only to make you feel better about having a bird...er, poop on you.

You are not supposed to walk under a ladder, but rather than this being actual bad luck I think it is more a safety issue.

Shoes on the table are bad luck (whether they have feet in them or not).

If you can make ivy grow in your home you have fidelity in your relationship.

Almost all dreams are about fears or sex, excepting rare spiritual or prophetic ones. Try keeping a notebook and pen beside the bed and recording your dreams as soon as you wake. You may learn much about yourself. This may work best when you wake naturally (i.e. not from an alarm or crying child), if you are lucky enough to do this once in awhile.

Dreaming of rough water means you feel out of control in some aspect of your life.

It's very nice to have representations of the elements in and about your home to help with balance in your life. Ideas for these include a small fountain, fish bowl, or water garden for water, candles, a fireplace, sun catcher, or even a fake fireplace for fire, plants, a Zen sandbox, or stones for earth, and incense, wind spinners, or wind chimes for air. Spirit or the fifth element might be represented by a lovely crystal or crystal ball. Use your imagination and sense of play to choose elemental representations and improve your spiritual richness.

Ants hate mint. Place bunches (thankfully taken), roots and all on cellophane or wax paper where they congregate to drive them away without pesticides.

Moths hate cedar. Protect your woollens with aromatic cedar boughs (thankfully cut) or commercially available cedar balls. Also peppercorns help drive them away and can be easily placed in garment pockets.

Mosquitoes and midges hate citrus and smoke. A "smudge pot" (Aunt Kitty's common use for her cauldron when it was not being used for magick) filled with gently smouldering herbs such as lemon balm, or a citronella candle will help keep them off without excessive use of poisonous bug repellents.

Poppets, pouches, and aromatic sachets can be filled out with baby powder or cotton balls so you need not use lots of an expensive ingredient, just a bit of oil or herbs, and still have your pouch nicely full.

Potpourri with a few drops of essential oil can make you house smell beautiful and help eliminate the need for expensive chemical air fresheners. Dry herbs such a lavender or mint, flowers such as roses or jasmine, and bits of lemon or orange peel. Add cinnamon sticks or cloves and the like. Plant matter should be hung upside down with an elastic band away from the sun for about a week. Make a blend that pleases you or make it as a kind of spell using perhaps love correspondences to make a mix for your mate's closet or prosperity correspondences to improve wealth in your home. Add 4-6 drops of pure essential oil and mix together in an attractive bowl or a container with holes in the lid. These last several months, and the oil can be replaced 3 or 4 times, about every six weeks to prolong the potpourri's life.

Clove oranges also make a fine aromatic, great for closets and drawers. Simply stick the sharp end of whole cloves into a regular orange in a pattern that pleases you. You can cover the whole orange if you like, but as cloves are rather expensive, I tend to just do several pentagrams or spirals. The orange will dry out but it will remain nicely scented for around six months.

A drop of honey or pinch of brown or cane sugar can be added to any spell to "keep things sweet" between two parties, perhaps in business or love spells.

Place clippings of your hair under the pillow, in the pockets of clothes, and in the shoes of a partner to keep you foremost in their minds.

You can empower makeup, hair products, soap, and so on to aid in a beauty or invisibility glamour. Charge them on your altar during your spell work.

Any tactile work such as cooking, sewing, gardening, construction, painting, carpentry and so on can be a spell or spiritual act. Focus on a mantra of intent with each stitch, hammer blow, etc, such as "more affection" with each brushstroke, or "less illness" with each counter-clockwise (widdershins) stir of the pot.

You can banish or remove negativity, worries, or someone or something while you bathe or clean. Sweep vigorously to chase away negativity, feel something being reduced as you scrub (like the song "I'm gonna wash that man right out of my hair").

Attract hummingbirds to your garden with bright red, orange, and hot pink flowers, especially those with a trumpet shape. In terms of hummingbird feeders, they like the type with a tiny perch so they may land while they eat, and a solution of 1 part dissolved brown sugar to 4 parts water. It is best not to use red food colouring in the solution, as studies have suggested the dye might be weakening their eggs. Get a feeder that is coloured red instead.

A watched pot never boils. This isn't strictly true, but if you stare at it, it seems to take forever. Of course, as soon as you walk away and forget about it, it boils and boils over at that. I don't recommend this.

If you kill a spider, it will rain. I don't like to kill them, so I don't know how well this one works. The "old aunts" swore by it. I have found setting them free outside has no discernable effect on the weather.

Butterflies like a large variety of nectar-bearing flowers and plants, including flowering herbs such as basil, nettles, milkweed, columbine, asters, bee balm, black-eyed susans, daisies, honeysuckle, lilac, lupines, purple coneflowers, sweet peas, thistles, queen anne's lace, clover, violets and zinnias. Since many of these are also noted spell correspondences they can serve a dual purpose when grown in your garden.

A slice of cool, raw onion or potato can be placed over a bee, wasp, or hornet sting to help draw out the stinger and ease the discomfort.

Morning glories and other climbing vines can be trained to climb strings tacked to walls. Make a pentagram or initial and spend a few moments every day or two gently winding the vines around the string when they are small. Makes a beautiful, living display.

In addition to being a fine stand in for graveyard dirt, mullein can be used to make many types of fish "dozy." Large quantities of fresh, crushed leaves can be added to a small pond or improvised fishing enclosure to make catching fish easier (and less traumatic for them, if, for instance, you are catching them as pets).

Cranberries are useful in spells to ease complaints of the bladder, and drinking large amount of cranberry juice will help cure a bladder infection.

Whole cloves or a small dab of oil of clove can be sucked on or rubbed into sore gums and help relieve a toothache.

Some folk clean out their hair brushes outside and leave the hair for the birds to use in their nest making, but this can cause headaches. It is better to offer them scraps of yarn or cloth. Try giving them some brightly coloured cloth and then looking for it later when it has been made into the nest. This is fun activity for young children.

When canning, jars and their lids can be sterilized in the dishwasher. So can sponges, dish scrubbers, toothbrushes and so on.

If you have a cold or flu it is an excellent time to replace your toothbrush.

If you would like to wear a pentagram or other magickal symbol but do not want to display it openly you could have it engraved on the inside of a ring or bracelet or on the back of a pendant. Additionally, words and symbols worn against the skin have power, which is no doubt part of the reason having the inside of wedding rings engraved with twinned initials or words is popular. You could also simply wear a five pointed star on clothing or jewellery. Jewellery depicting starfish, a natural five point star has lately become popular for women, and the five pointed star appears in many flags as well. A T-shirt with a small and simple five point star on it is a good and discreet choice for anyone.

Rain before 7am, shine before 11am. The same goes for tears:

if they come before 7am there will be happiness before 11am.

Peacocks and especially peacock feathers are considered extremely unlucky in my family tradition.

In order to help avoid "wells" in pillar or jar candles they should be burned one hour for every inch in diameter they are, especially the first time you use them.

Do not pass scissors directly from hand to hand to another person unless you want to sever or "cut" the relationship. Instead, place them on a surface for the other person to pick up. Knives do not have the same association, although if you give a knife to someone as a gift you should also give them a penny.

Many consider a woman to have the greatest access to magickal power during menstruation. Interestingly, it is also thought that a woman does not reach her greatest power until after menopause.

Vitamin E is wonderful for the skin and hair. Taking it in capsule form or eating lots of eggs will make your skin smoother and hair shinier. Try empowering the bottle of capsules on your altar. Burn orange or yellow candles and wave your hands clockwise over the open bottle, chanting something like "Better skin, shiny hair, all eyes on me as I become more fair" (fair in this case meaning good looking rather than pale).

Olive and other kitchen oils, eggs, or even mayonnaise make a fine hair masque. Pour about a cup over your hair, concentrating on the ends or other damaged areas, wrap your hair in towel or shower cap and sit in a warm place for as long as you can before washing it out with shampoo.

Lemon juice squeezed over hair before you sit in the sun will lighten it a little naturally.

Plain, prepared oatmeal makes a good face masque. Consider empowering it on your altar before use by circling your athame over it clockwise and visualizing the beneficial effects it will have. Then, spread about two tablespoons evenly over your face, place cucumber slices or ice cold wet teabags over your eyes and lie back for about twenty minutes. Rinse the oatmeal away with cool water and moisturize. Your skin will be soft and glowy.

Epsom salts added to bath water can reduce bloat. Dissolve about two cups under the hot tap as you run your bath, stir them up well and soak.

Try exfoliating your lips with a facecloth or soft toothbrush every couple of days and keeping them well moisturized with a natural balm. They will look and feel soft and smooth.

Caffeine is good for a headache. Try a cup of hot tea or coffee when you feel one coming on. In addition, hot coffee is good for wheezy breathing.

For a cold, try a eucalyptus-infused bath, taking Echinacea extract or zinc tablets, or try rubbing a mentholated grease such as Vicks on your feet at night and going to bed with wool socks on.

Honey has a variety of uses in health and magick. It keeps things sweet and is a fantastic ingredient in love cooking. It makes a good antiseptic when mixed with a little water for minor cuts and scrapes. Dabbed directly on pimples it makes them go away faster. It can also be mixed with egg whites and a little flour as a fine skin cleanser, and a spoonful slowly swallowed is great for a sore throat. White toothpaste dabbed on pimples before bed helps them dry up faster as well.

Gargling with a strong solution of salt and warm water is also excellent for a sore throat, but do not swallow, unless you need to induce vomiting for some reason.

If you don't mind the smell of white vinegar it works well

in a solution of 1 part vinegar to 3 parts hot water for washing windows, mirrors (magick or otherwise), gazing balls and other glass.

Consider incorporating a small dot somewhere in your signature so that you always know and can prove that it is you who has actually signed something (or not).

Large full moons that appear red (sometimes called Hunter's or Harvest Moons) are considered ill-omened by some, but in my family tradition they are said to mean a large change coming that may be positive or negative.

Think about boiling bones for an hour or two before giving them to your dog so there is less chance of a bone splinter becoming lodged in their throat.

Cats love to have a "perch," where they can look down on the room. Be it a cleared shelf, cabinet top, or special cat climber, some evidence suggests that unfixed tom cats will not spray in the house if they have such a perch, even in one room (although it is a good idea to spay or neuter house pets unless you are going to breed them).

Pet mice love peanut butter as much as or more than cheese.

In addition to chocolate, chicken skin can be very bad for dogs.

Broken egg shells' surrounding a garden helps to discourage slugs, and they will often drown if you place a dish with about an inch of beer in it near their path. Spray houseplants that are infested with whitefly with a weak solution of vodka and water. I dislike wounding or killing even humble bugs, but if it absolutely necessary I prefer a natural method of getting rid of them to harsh pesticides. The movement towards going green that is so popular today has been embraced by many witches for decades.

Wild animals such as deer like a "salt lick," a block of hard salt (which you can make yourself by getting a box of salt damp with water and then peeling the cardboard away) placed somewhere where they can have a lick without feeling too exposed. Makes for some good photo opportunities, as well as chance to observe wildlife and educate children as well as ourselves about the natural world.

In winter wild birds love a little augment to their diets. Young children will love to help make popcorn and cranberry garlands using a needle and thread or spreading peanut butter on pinecones or even fence posts for them.

It sounds odd and comical, but to discourage deer from eating your plants you can fill old pantyhose with clippings of your hair and tie them in the garden.

Collected feathers make nice representations of air, and can be knotted along the length of a cord to represent wishes. As each wish comes true (or manifests), unknot the feather and return it to nature. In addition, collected feathers of different colours make fine spell correspondences.

Be sure to bring home a little sand or earth or some stones from a place you wish to visit again. This could be on your vacation to Barbados, or it could be from the planter on the front walk of a girl's house who you'd like to date again.

If you don't like to iron (as I certainly don't) try hanging a wrinkled item near the shower while it is running (the hotter the better) with the bathroom door closed. Nine times out of ten this works fine.

Keep magickally empowered crystals or other stones in plain sight by incorporating them into plants, flower arrangements and centrepieces. Use larger ones as paper weights or simply curio objects.

Consider making a "nut tree" for Mabon or Yule to get in touch with the essence of the season. This is easily done by gluing acorns, walnuts, hazelnuts, almonds and other nuts still in their shells to a Styrofoam cone and adding a little glitter.

If you find a thread on your clothing you will soon receive an important letter (in this day in age it may mean an important email). The length of thread dictates the length of the letter.

If someone sees an eyelash on your face they should gently take it on their finger tip. Then you blow it off their finger while making a wish. This does not work if you find the eyelash yourself. The person holding the eyelash should lend their thoughts for a moment to making your wish come true.

Finally, the single adage I have always heard more than any other in my family was: 'Always follow your heart.' If you are ever in doubt about a large decision, whether in witchcraft or general life, it is best to listen to what your heart tells you and go where it leads you.

Lightning Source UK Ltd.
Milton Keynes UK

175853UK00001B/12/P